THE SIXTIES

A BLACK

CHRONOLOGY

by Norman Harris

The Black Resource Center
P.O. Box 6746
Athens, Georgia 30604

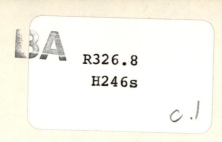
Library of Congress Catalog Number: 89-082691
ISBN 1-878531-00-X
Printed in the United States of America

Introduction

The purpose of this chronology is to provide the reader with a sense of what it was like to be an African-American in the sixties, a period from 1960 to 1974. I end the sixties in 1974 because the "unity without uniformity" ideology that linked revolutionary nationalists, cultural nationalists, and traditional Black Elected Officials (BEO's) was altered by the Little Rock National Political Convention held in 1974. "Unity without uniformity" was replaced by the concept of "ideological clarity," which functionally limited coalitions between various segments of the African-American activist community. In this fourteen-year period, many of America's promises of equality were tested by the Civil Rights Movement, the Black Power Movement, African-American involvement in Vietnam, and the Black Studies Movement.

For analytical clarity, I have divided the sixties into three phases: **Phase One, The Civil Rights Movement and Integration, 1960-1965; Phase Two, The Black Power Movement and Nationalism, 1966-1969; and Phase Three, Consolidating Gains, Minimizing Losses, 1970-1974.**

In **Phase One,** the dominant approach to social change was non-violent direct action based on an integrationist ideal which assumed that white Americans could be enlightened and thereby made to treat African-Americans with respect. This period ended with a number of important legal victories meant to ensure African-American rights.

In **Phase Two,** the dominant approach to social change was confrontational and it was based on a nationalist ideal which assumed that African-Americans had ultimate responsibility for changing the world. Under the eclectic banner of Black Power, a number of independent African-American economic, cultural, political, and educational institutions came into being.

During the **Phase Three,** there was a continuation of African-American attempts to institutionalize Black Power. Perhaps the most striking activity was the National Black Political Convention held in Gary, Indiana, in 1972.

The sixties ended with numerous independent African-American institutions and organizations struggling for survival and numerous African-American leaders jailed, murdered, discredited, or without a following. However, for African-Americans the legacy of the sixties is not one of failure and lost opportunities, but rather one of audacity, creativity and hope. During that fourteen-year period, a range of models and approaches to social change and a higher level of human life were tried with varying degrees of success. Perhaps the greatest legacy of that era is its illustration of the extent to which African-Americans can actually influence and shape the national agenda. The idealism of the sixties is a legacy that a new generation of African-American women and men must claim.

Phase One: 1960-1965
The Civil Rights Movement and Integration

The dual orientations of integration and nationalism have always co-existed in the African-American struggle for self-determination, but at given points in history one of the trends dominates. From 1960 until 1965, the Civil Rights Movement with its integrationist orientation was a dominant force. The goals of the Civil Rights Movement--though not always its methods--were consistent with national rhetoric concerning the need for African-Americans to enjoy democratic and constitutional rights. [1]

The decade began with African-American students launching "sit-in" demonstrations at segregated lunch counters. Shortly thereafter, the Congress of Racial Equality (CORE) conducted its "freedom rides" in an effort to desegregate public accommodations. The formation of the Student Non-Violent Coordinating Committee (SNCC) in 1960 indicated the pivotal and definitional role African-American students were to play in changing the face of American society during the sixties. At its inception, the integrationist ideology of SNCC was consistent with the Southern Christian Leadership Conference (SCLC), the organization that Dr. Martin Luther King, Jr., founded and the organization from which SNCC evolved.

An early contradiction in the Civil Rights Movement concerned the question of who would determine its goals and tactics. Given the fact that integration was a major goal of the Civil Rights Movement, this contradiction was an inevitable one as many well-meaning whites assumed that their vision of what African-Americans needed was accurate and defensible. Indeed, one of President Kennedy's early actions was an attempt to shift the "direct action" tactics of SNCC to less confrontational tactics aimed at voter-education. To this end, Kennedy was able to persuade two private philanthropic organizations, the Taconic Foundation and the Field Foundation, to fund voter education initiatives.

At a 1961 meeting, the majority of SNCC's membership argued that a shift from "direct action" to non-confrontational tactics to advance voter education was a "sell-out." Those who argued for "direct action" were in favor of registering African-Americans to vote, but they were opposed to individuals and organizations outside the movement telling them how best to advance those goals.

Mrs. Ella Baker, who played a key role in many dimensions of the movement during this phase of the sixties, was able to effect a compromise within SNCC whereby the organization would have a "direct action" branch that would use methods that might be viewed by others as confrontational, and a voter education branch that would use methods that were not confrontational. While the ideological and tactical dimensions of "direct action" and the gradualism that President Kennedy and others had in mind in using the term "voter education" are clearly debatable, the split of SNCC into two branches dramatically illustrated the central conflict of the Civil Rights Movement: who should determine the goals and tactics of that movement?

Efforts to desegregate public accommodations, institutions of higher education, and a variety of other public and private institutions during this period met with incredible resistance. Although the Interstate Commerce Commission banned racial discrimination on interstate buses and facilities in 1961, African-Americans had to "test" these laws in order to ultimately make them effective. Indeed, one of the reasons for the Albany (Georgia) Movement was the refusal of the local Greyhound station to allow African-Americans access to the "white" section of that facility.

The Council of Federated Organizations (COFO) in Mississippi had been trying to register African-Americans to vote since 1960, and they continued these efforts even after their offices in Greenwood, Mississippi were bombed in 1963, and even after the Voter Education Project decided to cut off funding efforts to register African-Americans to vote. Wiley Branton, the leader of the Voter Education Project, reasoned that white resistance to voter registration in Mississippi was so great that no amount of funds spent for that effort would effect change; he felt that the intervention of the federal government was necessary.

The Birmingham, Alabama campaign to register African-Americans to vote and to improve the quality of life for African-Americans also began in 1963. The response of many whites in Alabama was similar to that of terrorists: they bombed the homes of various African-Americans involved in the movement, burned churches, and generally sought to intimidate all those involved in the movement. Among the most devastating murders were those of four young black girls, killed by a bomb thrown into a Birmingham, Alabama church as they attended Sunday School.

One of the key issues of this phase of the sixties was the desegregation of public schools, and this issue was not limited to Southern states. For example, in 1963 over 200,000 students boycotted Chicago public schools to protest de facto segregation.

The "March on Washington" took place in 1963, and for many it was a crowning moment of the Civil Rights Movement. For it was there that Dr. Martin Luther King, Jr. delivered his famous "I Have A Dream" speech. However, some observers note that the politics and negotiations that structured the "March" served to emphasize the contradictions involved in the Civil Rights Movement. In general, the "March" went from its initial conception as a grassroots protest to one which was "sanitized," so much so that the speeches of participants (most notably that of John Lewis) had to be approved before being delivered. [2]

Also, in 1963 the Revolutionary Action Committee was formed, and, in some ways, it became a precursor for some of the Revolutionary Nationalist Organizations that were to either come into being or to regenerate during this phase, 1960-65.

Early in 1964, COFO decided that a "summer of activity" in Mississippi was needed to dramatize a range of problems confronting African-Americans in that state. The summer became known as "The Freedom Summer." African-American students, as well as white students from colleges and universities across the country volunteered to participate in the "Freedom Summer." As one measure of the political sophistication that COFO and SNCC had obtained, all of the volunteers were required to undergo training in the ideology and tactics of non-violent direct action protests. Importantly, some of those who volunteered were not accepted.

It is also important to note that the Freedom Summer represented one of the earliest instances of African-American creative artists (actors, set designers, and writers) consciously putting their craft into the service of the movement. Doris Derby, Gil Moses, and John O'Neal, who had created "The Free Southern Theater" in 1963 in Jackson, Mississippi, took their productions "to the people" during the Freedom Summer. [3] This notion of the role and purposes of African-American creative production was to reach an unparalleled level of sophistication during the second phase of the sixties (1966-1969) as the Black Arts Movement shaped and animated the efforts of numerous African-American artists. (More will be said about the Black Arts Movement in the next section. What is important here is to indicate the precedent "The Free Southern Theater" set for the Black Arts Movement.)

In 1964, a number of important laws were passed, and a number of African-Americans were elected to public office. The 24th Amendment to the Constitution was adopted and it prohibited the "denial or abridgment of the right to vote through the use of the poll tax, or other taxes"; the Civil Rights Act was passed, and it had provisions for the creation of the Equal Opportunity Commission. Congress launched its "War on Poverty" by passing the Economic Opportunity Act, which provided for such programs as Headstart, Upward Bound, and the College Work-Study Program. The Voting Rights Bill was passed. There were several notable victories in the area of electoral politics: Edward Brooke was elected as Attorney

General of Massachusetts and Leroy Johnson was elected to the Georgia State Senate. However, the greatest electoral victories were to occur after 1965, and in many ways those advances can be tied to the passage of the Voting Rights Bill.

As significant as these gains were, they did not immediately change the thinking of a great number of whites in the South. The Selma to Montgomery, Alabama, march was brutally stopped on the Edmund Pettus Bridge. Viola Liuzzo, a white Detroit housewife who participated in the march, was killed. Her murderers were ultimately convicted of violating her civil rights. The Reverend James Reeb, an African-American minister from Boston who participated in the march, was also killed. An Alabama jury acquitted those accused of murdering him. Among others who were killed during this era were James Chaney, Michael Shwerner, and Andrew Goodman, three Civil Rights workers whose bodies were found in Mississippi. Medgar Evers, field secretary of the Mississippi NAACP, was also murdered.

The use of the electoral process to advance African-American self-determination also took a more decidedly nationalist turn. For example, the Mississippi Freedom Democratic Party (MFDP) was founded in 1963. At the 1964 Democratic National Convention, the MFDP challenged the legitimacy of the all-white delegation from Mississippi, arguing that the white delegation was in no way representative of all the citizens in Mississippi. Through testimony, and a range of other evidence, MFDP demonstrated that African-Americans in Mississippi had been systematically left out of the electoral process. Concerned about not alienating white southern democrats, many northern white democrats, as well as many well-known African-American leaders, did not support MFDP's challenge. The fact that the challenge was not successful resulted in the radicalization of many of those involved in the Freedom Summer, the MFDP, and SNCC.

The Lowndes County (Alabama) Organization was founded during this period and it used as its symbol, the Black Panther. Black Nationalists in Michigan involved in the Freedom Now

Party placed 34 independent African-American candidates on the ballot.

Malcolm X, a minister in the Nation of Islam, was a popular and important leader for many African-Americans living in northern cities because of his ability to clearly and incisively deliver a message of African-American self-determination. **Muhammad Speaks**, the newspaper he helped found for the Nation of Islam, not only spread the Muslim religion as practiced by the Nation of Islam, it also added to Malcolm X's popularity. Malcolm X's comments that the assassination of President John F. Kennedy was a case of "chickens coming home to roost" was used as a basis for the Honorable Elijah Muhammad's decision to suspend Malcolm X from the Nation of Islam. Some observers of the Nation of Islam felt that Muhammad's decision represented his fear that Malcolm might overshadow him.

Malcolm X, a rhetorical and ideological model for many nationalists, was assassinated in 1965. A number of activists mark his assassination as a turning point in their lives, an event which radicalized them. His death came at a time when he was putting together the Organization of Afro-American Unity, which was modeled on the Organization of African Unity.

During Phase One, African-American involvement in the war in Vietnam was generally viewed in a positive light. Among many African-Americans stateside, as well as among many African-Americans fighting, the war in Vietnam provided an opportunity for African-Americans to convince whites of their patriotism and worth. For this was the first American war in which there were no segregated units as a matter of military policy. As late as 1966, only 35% of African-Americans polled opposed the war in Vietnam. [4]

The period of 1960 until 1965 was phenomenal in terms of the sacrifices and successes of individuals and organizations involved in the Civil Rights Movement. These activists managed to focus national attention on the absence of democratic and constitutional rights of African-Americans in the South, and their actions led to enactment of several statutes which now provide the legal space for African-Americans to maneuver for empowerment.

Phase Two: 1966-1969
The Black Power Movement and Nationalism

During this period, the dominant orientation for African-American self-determination was nationalist, and in some ways that orientation resulted from unresolved conflicts within the Civil Rights Movement as to who would determine the goals and tactics of that movement. Indeed many of the individuals involved in the Black Power Movement had been involved in the Civil Rights Movement and had been radicalized by both the ideological and tactical limitations of integrationist thought.

In 1966 James Meredith was shot before completing his "March Against Fear" from Memphis, Tennessee, to Jackson, Mississippi. His shooting outraged many Americans and a decision was made by the civil rights community and the emerging nationalist community that the march would be completed. During the course of the march, Willie Ricks, an Atlanta activist and SNCC member, chanted the slogan Black Power. At a speech made during the march, Stokely Carmichael, the president of SNCC, said African-Americans had to stop asking for things, and start securing **Black Power.** The slogan galvanized a generation, touching a complex of feelings and ideas that could not be touched by the rhetoric of the Civil Rights Movement.

In general, Black Power came to mean the empowerment of African-American communities in accordance to the goals and wishes of those communities. A tremendous amount of attention was given to "Nation Building," which came to mean the creation and support of independent African-American institutions. Many of the political institutions such as CORE and, most notably, SNCC that had come into existence prior to the Black Power era, invited whites to leave their ranks. The African-American members of these organizations reasoned that African-Americans had to be at the forefront of the African-American struggle for self-determination. [5]

Disparate activities were carried out under the banner of Black Power. In many ways the Black Power Movement became associated with a set of symbols (the clenched fist, the dashiki, the "natural," African names to replace our slave names, etc.) that were not consistently tied to specific actions and the building of institutions responsible to the various African-American communities. Therefore it became relatively easy for unprincipled African-Americans and whites intent on maintaining power to use those symbols in a variety of ways not tied to the empowerment of African-American communities. Thus, many of the symbols were reduced to commodities (which after all is a central function of a capitalist society) and thereby robbed of much of their cultural and political impetus. Indeed, during his 1968 run for the presidency, Richard Nixon offered a definition of Black Power as an essentially economic concept called "Black Capitalism." While many of those involved in the Black Power Movement would acknowledge the need for that movement to advance actions meant to create an economic base over which African-Americans exercised control, few would want that base to be a duplication of "white capitalism." One of the major concerns of the Black Power Movement was the idea that new institutions had to be based on an African-American worldview.

Established Civil Rights organizations such as the NAACP, the Urban League, and SCLC vigorously condemned Black Power. For these organizations, the combination of the words Black and Power was as improbable as it was frightening. The integrationist goals and strategies of these organizations simply made it impossible for them to think of a world defined from an African-American perspective. [6]

Just as the Civil Rights Movement with its integrationist ideology failed to deal with the relationship between economic rights and democratic rights in a capitalist society, the Black Power Movement with its nationalist ideology also failed to deal with this relationship. To be sure, the Nguzo Saba (seven principles) of the US organization did have as its fourth principle, ujamaa (cooperative economics); however, the contradiction of practicing cooperative economics in a capitalist economy was not systematically addressed during this era. Perhaps the central conflict between revolutionary nationalists and cultural nationalists, which was to become so intense in the third phase of the sixties, 1970-74, centered on the question of how best to understand and alter African-Americans' relationship to this country's productive forces.

The Black Panther Party, founded in 1966, had as one of its major purposes, "policing the police," trailing them through the Oakland, California community to make sure that they did not abuse its African-American citizens. For many observers, the Panthers were the quintessential revolutionary nationalist organization. The Panthers were often in conflict with US, the quintessential cultural nationalist organization.

While a number of observers asserted that conflicts between the two organizations were either the result of warring egos, or the work of FBI infiltrators intent on destroying the African-American movement, there were fundamental differences between the way revolutionary nationalists and cultural nationalists viewed America and, consequently, the way they thought of changing America.

The Black Panther Party, particularly under the leadership of Eldridge Cleaver, viewed America as being composed of competing classes. Racism, they felt, obscured this fact; the elimination of racism would allow the working class to unite and overthrow the ruling class. On the other hand, US assumed that America was a pluralist society composed of competing ethnic groups. From their perspective, social advancement for African-Americans could occur only after they solidified around a clear set of values. As indicated above, these ideological differences between the Black Panthers and US were exacerbated by the systematic infiltration and disruption of both organizations through the Federal Bureau of Investigation COINTELPRO program. [7]

During this period, a number of independent African-American cultural organizations came into being: Spirit House in Newark; the Organization of Black American Culture in

Chicago; the Black House in San Francisco; the New School for Afro-American Thought in Washington, D.C.; Broadside Press in Detroit; and Black Art South in New Orleans. These organizations and others like them contributed to what became known as the Black Arts Movement, the "spiritual sister of the Black Power Movement." [8]

In general, the Black Arts Movement redefined African-American artistic creation through the use of images, ideas, and modes of expression derived from the Black World experience. Poetry owed more to the rhythmic explosions of James Brown than to attempts to reproduce Shakespearean sonnets. African-American drama turned its focus to instructing the various African-American communities, and this was a departure from much of the integrationist drama that had preceded the Black Arts Movement.

In addition to the creative outpourings of the Black Arts Movement, a number of important publications appeared: Harold Cruse's **The Crisis of the Negro Intellectual**, and John A. Williams' novel, **The Man Who Cried I Am** are two such important publications.

The struggle for self-determination that fueled the Black Power movement affected relationships between African-American women and men. The question of who should lead the Black Power Movement exposed the male chauvinism among such organizations as the Nation of Islam, US, and the Congress of African People.   In general, it was felt that black men should lead the struggle, and that black women should play supportive roles. In some instances, a legitimate concern of some activists about genocide being directed at African-Americans was used by some individuals to gain sexual advantage over black women: the women were encouraged to "have a baby for the revolution." To be sure, a number of African-American women bought into this ideology too. Relationships between African-American women and men remain a topic of intense debate. [9]

Racial rebellions in numerous American cities were one of the defining elements of this part of the sixties. In most of the rebellions, the police were seen as an occupying force that routinely brutalized the African-American community. Police actions sparked racial rebellions in Watts, Newark, Detroit, Cleveland, and in many other cities. To be sure, the conditions for rebellions preceded the police "spark" that ignited them. The Kerner Commission was to report that America was moving "towards two separate societies, one black, one white, separate and unequal."

In 1967, African-American students at Howard University, a predominantly African-American university in Washington, D.C., demanded that their experiences and culture be made a part of the curriculum. Within a year of this protest, African-American students at a number of prestigious universities made similar demands. The result was the creation of Black Studies as a discipline with the first Black Studies Program being created in 1968 at San Francisco State University with Dr. Nathan Hare as its director.

The way African-Americans viewed the war in Vietnam underwent a fundamental change. A national poll conducted in 1969 indicated that 56% of all African-Americans opposed the war in Vietnam. During this phase, many African-American soldiers fighting in Vietnam viewed white commanding officers and peers as more of an enemy than the North Vietnamese. Thus, African-American soldiers created their own self-defense organizations within Vietnam; one such organization took as its name the MauMaus, the name of a Kenyan liberation front associated with ending colonialism in that African nation. [10]

The world and the nation were stunned by the assassination of Dr. Martin Luther King, Jr. Riots broke out in cities across the country, as many sought some way to vent their anger at his death. Dr. King's funeral rivaled that of a head of state.

Some of the numerous victories in electoral politics that occurred during this phase of the sixties follow: Richard Gordon Hatcher was elected mayor of Gary, Indiana; Carl B. Stokes was elected mayor of Cleveland, Ohio; Robert Clark became the first

African-American elected to the Mississippi legislature since Reconstruction; Floyd McCree was elected mayor of Flint, Michigan; and Shirley Chisholm defeated James Farmer and became the first African-American woman to sit in Congress.

This period of the sixties (1966-1969) was characterized by a general shift towards nationalism in all aspects of the African-American quest for self-determination. Electoral and protest politics were affected, as were artistic and cultural activities. Perhaps the most lasting legacy of this part of the sixties is the reversal of images in terms of standards of beauty and ways of thinking about what is possible. In effect, this part of the sixties rekindled a feeling of power and audacity among African-Americans.

Phase Three: 1970-1974
Consolidating Gains, Minimizing Losses

The third phase of the Movement was characterized by a continuation of attempts to institutionalize the ideas of the Black Power Movement, a continuation of the police attack on the Black Panther Party and other African-American organizations, and a continuation of the "ideological debate" between revolutionary and cultural nationalists.

Organizations founded during this period represented not only the dual thrusts of the nationalist movement (revolutionary and cultural), but they also represented a regeneration of aspects of the Civil Rights Movement and a renewed focus on electoral politics as a basis to advance African-American self-determination. Jesse Jackson's Operation PUSH (People United to Save Humanity), which was founded in 1971, represented a continuation of some of the goals of the Civil Rights Movement, particularly in terms of trying to convince white elected officials to be more accountable to their African-American constituency. Importantly, Operation PUSH focused more attention on both the economic plight and power of African-Americans, and this represented a continuation of the direction that Dr. Martin Luther King Jr. was beginning to travel at the time of his assassination.

In 1970, Malcolm X University in North Carolina and Peoples College in Nashville, Tennessee, emerged. For many observers, these institutions and others like them represented the natural evolution of the Black Studies Movement, and the discussion of a "Black University," which was the focus of two issues of **Negro Digest** in 1969. It is also important to note that at the beginning of this phase of the sixties, there were over 500 African-American Studies Programs nationwide, but by the end of this phase there were approximately 200 such programs. For most observers, this drop in number was tied directly to waning influence of African-Americans on the political landscape of this

16

country.

Black Elected Officials (BEO's) increased tremendously during this period. In addition to the mayoral victories in cities like Gary, Indiana and Cleveland, Ohio that occurred in the previous phase, major cities like Detroit, Michigan, Newark, New Jersey, and Atlanta, Georgia also elected African-American mayors. Most of these men came to power by galvanizing the black vote through programs and promises that indicated that the African-American community would finally have a voice in determining how their cities would be run. It should be noted that in many instances the mayors of these cities had openly courted the activist community for support. The ability of the nationalist (revolutionary and cultural) community to work with the bourgeois middle-class community suggested a level of development that was more mature than that which structured aspects of the Black Power Movement.

This new level of development attained its most eloquent expression at the National Black Political Convention held in Gary, Indiana in 1972. This convention was more representative of the various segments which constitute the African-American community than any of the various conventions of organizations such as the NAACP, CORE, the Congress of African People, and the Urban League. The thrust of the convention was the creation of a platform which any candidate wishing African-American support had to endorse. In his opening remarks, Richard Gordon Hatcher, the mayor of Gary and one of the convention's conveners, said that "preoccupation with power in the absence of ideology is the prelude to betrayal." As it turned out, Hatcher was right inasmuch as many of the BEO's and aspiring BEO's ignored the convention's platform and worked diligently to cut individual deals at the Democratic National Convention of 1972.

By 1974, when the second National Convention was held--this time in Little Rock, Arkansas--it was painfully clear that the "unity without uniformity" ideal which had structured the first convention had dissipated. Many BEO's felt that they no longer needed the nationalist community to get re-elected and subsequently set out to secure loyalty among African-American voters, using time honored methods of rewards and punishments. The nationalists, for their part, had been engaged in an increasingly bitter debate about the role of race and class in determining social change: the revolutionary nationalists felt socialism offered the only realistic alternative to capitalism, and that Marxism (in one or the other of its permutations) offered the most systematic critique of capitalist society; cultural nationalists felt that cooperative economics offered the best alternative for African-Americans in a capitalist society, and that a pluralist analysis of America, in which racial and ethnic groups remained loyal to defending and developing their group interests, was the best way to understand American society.

Easily, the most fantastic conversion during this phase of the sixties, was Amiri Baraka's move from cultural nationalism to revolutionary nationalism. In a long essay entitled, "Why I Changed My Ideology," he attempted to justify his move, by arguing that cultural nationalism lacked the analytical capacity to critique capitalism and to project alternatives to the current system; further, Baraka argued, socialism was more in line with the way other oppressed people in the world were ending their oppression. However, a number of cultural nationalists who were Baraka advocates, disagreed with his ideological shift. Chief among his critics was Haki Madhubuti, who asserted in an essay ("The Latest Purge: The Attack on Black Nationalism and Pan-Africanism by the New Left, the Sons and Daughters of the Old Left") that for many activists, the "attack" on nationalism was an emotional response, in effect, a love for whites.

This very volatile period of African-American intellectual history is in need of systematic treatment from a variety of points of view. Here I wish to point out that the way the ideological debate between cultural and revolutionary nationalists was conducted made it easier than it would have otherwise been for a range of government agents to infiltrate and disrupt a variety of African-American organizations. Such disruption was in keeping with official U.S. government policy towards African-American leaders and organizations that were labeled a "threat" to national security. Certainly, no organization suffered the systematic and relentless attention of the government policing agents as did the Black Panther Party. Perhaps the most brutal example were the murders of Illinois Panther members Fred Hampton and Mark Clark by Chicago area policing agents. Their bodies were riddled with hundreds of rounds of bullets as they slept.

When African-American leaders were not killed, they were often imprisoned on "trumped up charges," and they became known as "political prisoners"--individuals whose only crime was being too assertively Black at the wrong time and at the wrong place. Ron Karenga, Ruchell MaGhee, George Jackson, Angela Davis, Muhammad Ahmed, the Wilmington Ten, and countless others were political prisoners during this phase of the sixties. As a measure of how widespread this phenomenon was, **The Black Scholar** devoted two separate issues to the plight of the "Black Prisoner."

Before the war in Vietnam came to an end, the number of African-American soldiers killed in Vietnam increased dramatically; indeed, the disproportionate number of casualties and the kind of treatment that African-American soldiers received from white commanding officers led the Congressional Black Caucus, which was formed in 1971, to conduct a study of the Black soldier's status. Among their conclusions was that African-American soldiers who showed any kind of "Black Consciousness" were subject to more hazardous duty, poorer treatment on the part of commanding officers, and dishonorable discharges than were African-American soldiers who did not show such consciousness.

Perhaps the greatest challenge this last phase of the sixties leaves, is how to create mechanisms that allow the fullest opportunity for all African-Americans to contribute to their various communities. Increasingly, African-American leaders and politicians view that segment of the African-American community which has the least (the underclass) in ways similar to the way all African-Americans have been historically viewed by whites.

Conclusion

Because it was a period of volatility, idealism, and audacity, the sixties contains lessons for current and future generations. This is not to suggest that the sixties "jes grew," but that many of the opportunities and contradictions which characterize African-American life came dramatically to the forefront during this era.

Future research concerning the sixties and African-Americans might seek to deal with the following set of questions: What is an African-American vision of the world? What is an African-American institution? Who should support African-American institutions? On what should African-American women and men base their relationships? What are the roles of **race** and **class** in understanding the opportunities and problems facing African-Americans? Are the roles of **race** and **class** unchanging?

These questions flow from my essay, and are intended to be more suggestive than definitive.

NOTES

1. One measure of public sentiment concerning current events can be found in the news and popular magazines of a given era. Accordingly, the following articles are useful indicators as to the positive ways in which some of the northern white media viewed the Civil Rights Movement: "Fights Not Over," **Commonweal,** 5 May 1961, p. 141; "For Negro Rights," **America,** 13 May 1961, pp. 266-67; "Inevitable Process," **Time,** 14 June 1963, pp. 24-25; "Right to Vote a Must," **U.S. News and World Report,** 18 June 1963, pp. 110-12; "What Congress Plans to Do About Negro Rights," **U.S. News and World Report,** 14 March 1960, pp. 46-48; "Within the Framework," **Time,** 8 February 1960, p. 29.

2. For an incisive discussion of the "behind the scenes" maneuvering that structured the "March on Washington," see Michael Thelwell's **Duties, Pleasures and Conflicts** (Amherst: University of Massachusetts Press, 1987). Cleve Seller's **River of No Return** (New York: William Morrow, 1973), provides a personal account of the way the "March on Washington" affected SNCC members who had been active in a variety of "movement" activities. Other excellent sources are Robert Brisbane's **Black Activism** (Valley Forge, PA.: Judson Press, 1971); Clayborne Carson's **In Struggle: SNCC and the Black Awakening of the Sixties** (Cambridge: Harvard University Press, 1981); and Manning Marable's **Race Reform and Rebellion** (Jackson: University Press of Mississippi, 1984).

3. For a discussion of the Free Southern Theater see "Mirror of the Movement: The History of the **Free Southern Theater** as a Microcosm of the Civil Rights and the Black Power Movements" (Unpublished Dissertation: Emory University, 1988), by Clarissa Myrick-Harris.

4. For discussions of African-American involvement in the war in Vietnam see **Connecting Times: The Sixties in Afro-American Fiction** (Jackson, Mississippi: University Press of Mississippi, 1988) by Norman Harris.

5. A beginning source for any discussion of Black Power is the book by Stokely Carmichael and Charles V. Hamilton, **Black Power** (New York: Vintage Books, 1967). For discussions about the way whites viewed Black Power, see the following: "Grasping at Chaos," **Nation,** 27 November 1967, pp. 547-48; "Here Lies Integration," **National Review,** 27 December 1966, pp. 1305-06; "Major Turning Point Against the Negro Movement," **U.S. News and World Report,** 15 August 1966, p. 46; "Racial Crisis: A Consensus," **Newsweek,** 21 August 1967, pp. 16-17.

6. In addition to the books by Brisbane, Carson, and Thelwell noted above, the reader can also refer to the following periodical references to get a sense of how Americans wedded to the integrationist approach of African-American empowerment viewed the conflict between established civil rights organizations and nationalists organizations on the issue of Black Power: "New Racism, Emphasis on Black Power," **Time,** 1 July 1966, pp. 11-13; "Pharaoh's Lessons: Fighting Among Themselves," **Time,** 9 September 1966, p. 22; and Carl T. Rowan, "Crisis in Civil

Rights Leadership," **Ebony**, November 1966, pp. 27-30.

7.   For a discussion of this phenomenon, see Nelson Blackstock's **COINTELPRO: The FBI's Secret War on Political Freedom** (New York: Vintage Books, 1984).

8.   Two excellent anthologies of the Black Arts era follow: Leroi Jones and Larry Neal, eds. **Black Fire** (New York: William Morrow, 1968); Addison Gayle, ed. **The Black Aesthetic** (Garden City, New York: Doubleday, 1971). Carolyn Fowler's **Black Arts and Black Aesthetics** (Atlanta, Georgia: First World Foundation Publication, 1976) is a definitive bibliography of this era.

9.   Delores Aldridge's edited volume, **Black Male-Female Relationships** (Dubuque, Iowa: Kendall/Hunt Publishing Company, 1989), covers a variety of structural and ideological issues affecting relationships between African-American women and men.

10.   See Clyde Taylor, ed. **Vietnam and Black America** (New York: Doubleday, 1973); Robert Mullen's **Blacks in America's Wars** (New York: Monad Press, 1973); and Wallace Terry's **Bloods** (New York: Random House, 1984).

Phase One: 1960-1965
The Civil Rights Movement
and Integration

(1960) Joseph McNeil, David Richmond, Franklin McCain, and Izell Blair, all students at North Carolina Agricultural and Technical College in Greensboro, North Carolina, "sit-in" at the "whites only section" of the Woolworth lunch counter, thereby launching what some historians call the "second reconstruction."

(1960) Mississippi Governor Ross Barnett refuses to meet with the Council of Federated Organizations (COFO) to discuss ways of improving the quality of life for African-Americans, saying, "Nothing you ask, am I willing to do." Aaron Henry led the federation, which was composed of African-American members of the Elks, Masons, school teachers, and other members of the African-American community.

(1960) African-American students from North Carolina College and white students from Duke University attempt to integrate a local facility by "sitting-in."

(1960) At a meeting attended by over 500 students representing Fisk University, Tennessee State University, Meharry Medical College, and the American Baptist Seminary, a decision is made to begin "sit-in" protests in Nashville. Marion Berry, James Lawson, and John Lewis assume leadership roles in this protest. Their protests are met with violence, including the pushing of lighted cigarettes into the backs of the African-American women who participated in the protest.

(1960) Julian Bond, Lonnie King, and Joe Pierce inform Morehouse President Dr. Benjamin E. Mays of their plans to

23

involve Atlanta area African-American students in the sit-in protest.

(1960) The Georgia General Assembly enacts "anti-trespass laws" in an effort to make "sit-ins" illegal.

(1960) African-American students from Alabama State University stage a sit-in demonstration at the state capital of Montgomery, and within a week's time angry whites attack the students and other African-Americans. Alabama's Governor, John Paterson, continues a tradition of racist politics by blaming the victims of racism, asserting that he could not offer protection to blacks who "provoke whites."

(1960) Gwendolyn Brooks combines free verse and lyric poems in her book of poetry, **The Bean Eaters.** Brooks' poetry would later win for her the Pulitzer Prize and the honorific title of poet-laureate of Illinois.

(1960) On their way to protest a meeting at the state capitol, over 1,000 African-Americans in Arkansas are stopped by police officials; there are fistfights between African-American activists and racist whites.

(1960) President Eisenhower endorses the creation of "biracial conferences" in southern cities as a means to ease racial tensions.

(1960) Felton Turner is kidnapped in Houston; he is beaten and the letters KKK are carved across his chest and stomach. His kidnapping appears to be a retaliation for a sit-in by more than 100 Texas Southern University students.

(1960) The home of a black Nashville attorney for the NAACP and city councilman is destroyed by a dynamite bomb. Although Councilman Lobby and his family escape injury, many students at nearby Meharry Medical College are injured by flying glass that shattered at the medical school as a result of the explosion. (This kind of terrorism was repeated in Nashville and other cities throughout the South during the sixties.)

(1960) Two hundred and twelve delegates, of which one hundred and forty-five were students, attend a Southern Christian Leadership Conference (SCLC) on student "sit-ins" that is spearheaded by Ella Baker. One of the points Mrs. Baker makes is that the protests have to be about "more than a hamburger"--referring here to the desegregation of lunch counters.

(1960) President Eisenhower signs the Voting Rights Act of 1960, but its provisions are so cumbersome that a stronger provision is necessary.

(1960) Bob Moses goes South to work in the movement, and commences an important relationship in Cleveland, Mississippi, with Amzie Moore, the local NAACP leader.

(1960) The Honorable Elijah Muhammad, the leader of the Nation of Islam, calls for the establishment of an all-black state. At various points during the decade, this call is made by different nationalist organizations.

(1960) Nelson Rockefeller, the governor of New York, tells Urban League conventioneers that the sit-ins are an "inspiring example." (Slightly more than a decade later, Rockefeller would be roundly criticized for his less than inspiring handling of the Attica Prison uprising.)

(1960) The student delegates to the SCLC-sponsored conference meet again and adopt the name, the Student Non-Violent Coordinating Committee (SNCC). The leadership was to consist of a delegate from each of the sixteen southern states, and from the District of Columbia.

(1960) Martin Luther King, Jr. is transferred to the Reidsville State Prison for participating in a "sit-in" at Rich's Department store. His participation and subsequent arrest violate the terms of his probation.

(1960) President-elect Kennedy names Andrew Hatcher his

associate press secretary, making Hatcher one of the highest ranking black appointees in the Kennedy administration.

(1960) The Kennedy administration defines the struggle in the South in terms of enfranchisement, and thereby encourages the participation of private foundations and business in the registration of potential African-American voters. Accordingly, the Field Foundation donates $100,000 to black voter registration efforts; the Southern Regional Council becomes active in these efforts, as does the Taconic Foundation.

(1960) Membership in the Nation of Islam reportedly reaches more than 100,000.

(1961) The University of Mississippi denies James Meredith admission.

(1961) Whites riot at the University of Georgia because they do not want two African-American students admitted to the university; however, a court order reinstates the two students.

(1961) Robert Weaver, who has a Ph.D. from Harvard and is an expert on housing, becomes the Administrator for the Housing and Home Finance Agency.

(1961) The Congress of Racial Equality (CORE) begins its "Freedom Rides" in an effort to desegregate interstate travel.

(1961) Bob Moses is invited to McComb, Mississippi, by C.C. Bryant, the head of the McComb NAACP; Moses is to spearhead the McComb voter registration drive.

(1961) The Taconic Foundation and the Field Foundation, through the auspices of the National Student Association, argue the need for voter education as opposed to direct-action demonstrations; Tim Jenkins, the black vice president of the organization advances this line of reasoning at the SNCC June meeting.

(1961) At their meeting at the Highlander Folk School in

Tennessee, most SNCC members feel a focus on voter education is a diversion created by the establishment. Members who feel this way fear that SNCC might end up "selling out to the establishment." Mrs. Ella Baker intervenes, suggesting two branches of SNCC, one to continue the "direct action" work and another to deal with voter education.

(1961) Moses and several other African-Americans are "savagely" beaten by local police when they show up in Liberty, Mississippi to register blacks to vote.

(1961) Bobby Seale enrolls as a student at Merrit College in Oakland, California; within a year after his enrollment he meets fellow student, and "brother in struggle," Huey Newton.

(1961) Herbert Lee, an African-American farmer who worked voter registration in Liberty, Mississippi, is killed by white state representative, E.H. Hunt. Claiming self-defense, Hunt is never tried.

(1961) The Voter Education Leadership training center opens in Dorchester, Georgia.

(1961) Southern Regional Council reports that desegregation of public accommodations had been achieved in more than 100 southern cities and towns.

(1961) The Interstate Commerce Commission bars racial discrimination on interstate buses and facilities.

(1961) President Kennedy praises the peaceful integration of four high schools in Atlanta, Georgia.

(1961) Thurgood Marshall is appointed by President Kennedy as a Judge of the Second Circuit Court of Appeals.

(1961) SNCC sends Charles Jones, Robert Sherrod, and Cordell Reagan to Albany, Georgia, to set up a field office in the black community.

(1961) In McComb, Mississippi, Bob Moses and nineteen other SNCC workers are charged with "breach of peace" for demonstrating for democratic rights.

(1961) In Seattle, Washington, CORE members picket a local supermarket and secure employment for five African-Americans.

(1961) Eli Brumfield is killed by Mississippi police because they think he is a SNCC worker.

(1961) The "Albany Movement" is formed at a meeting called by Dr. William C. Anderson, a black osteopath.

(1961) Youth members of the Albany, Georgia, NAACP test the antidiscriminatory ruling of the Interstate Commerce Commission and are turned away from the bus station.

(1961) Because over 500 African-Americans in Albany are either in jail or out on bond, the city leaders agree to the establishment of a "bi-racial commission" to hear about and deal with black complaints.

(1961) King responds to the call from Albany, speaks to an overflow crowd at Shiloh Baptist Church, leads a march, and is arrested. King vows to stay in jail, but city officials announce a truce; King posts bail, and leaves jail. For some younger members of the Civil Rights Movement, this act undercuts his legitimacy.

(1961) W.E.B. Dubois publishes **Worlds of Color**, the third installment of his **Black Flame Trilogy**.

(1961) Many black citizens of Albany suffer harassment, police brutality, and other indignities as a result of their support of the Albany Movement.

(1961) Leroi Jones (Amiri Baraka) publishes **Preface to a Twenty Volume Suicide Note**. (This volume of poetry would be the last Jones would write within the traditions of standard or accepted poetic discourse. As the sixties progressed, his works, both structurally and thematically, would be shaped by the Black Power and Black Arts movements.)

(1961) Langston Hughes publishes **The Best of Simple.** (This collection remains a standard for individuals interested in the African-American perspective on a variety of issues being rendered in the framework of a logic and in a vernacular that shows fidelity to the African-American experience.)

(1962) African-Americans in Albany, Georgia, renew their demands for justice and do not ask for King's assistance.

(1962) The American Negro Leadership Conference on Africa is formed; its major goal is to force America to condemn imperialism directed against Africa.

(1962) Students at Southern University (Baton Rouge, Louisiana), the largest African-American state university in the South, protest the expulsion of students who participated in sit-in demonstrations. Subsequent student demonstrations result in Southern University officials closing the university down, thereby satisfying various white governmental officials who saw black schools as a potential breeding ground for radicalism.

(1962) At the urging of President Kennedy, the Taconic Foundation and the Edgar Stern Foundation commit several hundred thousand dollars to the Southern Regional Council to establish the Voter Education Project (VEP) for two years under the leadership of Wiley A. Branton.

(1962) Julian Mayfield publishes the first issue of the **African Review,** an important journal of the era.

(1962) SCLC decides to support the Reverend Fred Shuttlesworth of Birmingham, Alabama, with a "massive direct action campaign intended to end segregation."

(1962) COFO is given a $14,000 grant to conduct voter education in Mississippi.

(1962) Governor Ross Barnett of Mississippi blocks the admission of James Meredith to the University of Mississippi, saying that state troopers would arrest him if he tried to enroll.

(1962) In Sasser, Georgia, white racists burn down two African-American churches, thereby continuing the terrorist attacks of whites on African-American institutions that play a positive role in the Civil Rights Movement.

(1962) Federal marshals escort Meredith into the University of Mississippi, and are attacked by white racists. The attack prompts President Kennedy to send over 300 soldiers to "Ole Miss." Prior to the arrival of the troops, 2 people are killed, 166 marshals and 210 demonstrators are injured.

(1962) Edward Brooke becomes the first African-American elected Attorney-General for Massachusetts.

(1962) Leroy Johnson is the first African-American elected to the Georgia State Senate.

(1962) President Kennedy bans racial discrimination in federally financed housing, but the ban has little impact on changing the nation's discriminatory housing patterns.

(1962) Augustus F. Hawkins of Los Angeles, California, is elected to Congress, thereby becoming the first African-American congressman from the West.

(1962) White Mississippi political officials use the distribution of surplus food as a basis to discourage African-Americans from pursuing democratic rights. For example, residents of Senator Eastland's Sunflower county, had to get "reasonable persons" to countersign their applications for "surplus food."

(1962) James Baldwin's **Another Country** is published. (As the decade progresses, Baldwin's essays, and his play, "Blues for Mr. Charlie," establish him as an important interpreter of cultural and racial events.)

(1962) Malcolm X's personal influence begins to grow, particularly through **Muhammad Speaks,** the newspaper he helped to establish.

(1962) The African-American poets Tom Dent, Calvin Hernton, David Henderson, Ishmael Reed, Askia Muhammad Toure, Joe Johnson, Lorenzo Thomas, and Norman Pritchard meet weekly in New York's Lower East Side and become known as the Umbra Poet's Workshop.

(1963) The Revolutionary Action Committee (later to become Revolutionary Action Movement or RAM) comes into being. From its inception, the group has a close relationship with Robert F. Williams who was a leader of the Monroe, North Carolina NAACP, but he fell from favor with the national office of the NAACP for advocating self-defense. Williams starts the Deacons of Defense.

(1963) Romare Bearden and Norman Lewis found an organization called the **Spiral Group** and assert that the racial conflict in America makes it necessary for them to paint only in black and white.

(1963) Mississippi Governor Ross Barnett is telegrammed by Attorney General Robert Kennedy and told that the Federal government expects the state of Mississippi to protect individuals participating in the Voter Education Project.

(1963) COFO offices in Greenwood, Mississippi, are set afire, destroying all the organization's equipment and records.

(1963) The Federal government reaches an agreement with officials in Greenwood, Mississippi, which calls for it to drop "injunctive" proceedings against the city in return for the city's guaranteeing safe voter registration for its African-American citizens.

(1963) SNCC members operating in the Mississippi Delta are unfazed by the agreement between the Federal government and Greenwood, Mississippi. They continue their attempts to register African-Americans. Chief among these activists is Bob Moses.

(1963) The Birmingham, Alabama campaign begins. The white response is one of terrorism in which the homes of various Birmingham African-Americans involved in the campaign are bombed.

(1963) Assistant Attorney General Burke Marshall, Secretary of Defense Robert McNamara, and Treasurer Secretary C. Douglas Dillon reach an agreement with Birmingham's elected officials and corporate leaders that calls for non-discriminatory hiring practices.

(1963) The idea of a "March on Washington" begins to take shape. The tone and thrust of the march, which is one of massive civil disobedience, is altered as a result of concerns by the NAACP and the Urban League.

(1963) Law officials in Mississippi unleash a wave of repression against Civil Rights activists: 72 African-Americans are arrested in Biloxi; Willie Joe Lovett, a 23 year-old activist, is killed; Fannie Lou Hamer and other Civil Rights activists are savagely beaten in Winona for attempting to register to vote.

(1963) Medgar Evers, the field secretary of the Mississippi NAACP, is killed.

(1963) Malcolm X learns of Elijah Muhammad's adultery and interviews the two women whose children he fathered. He discovers that Elijah Muhammad sees Malcolm as a dangerous man, a threat to his influence. Later in the year, Elijah Muhammad uses Malcolm X's statement that President Kennedy's assassination was a case of "chickens coming home to roost" as a basis to suspend Malcolm X from the Nation of Islam.

(1963) The March on Washington takes place. For many, it is the crowning moment of the Civil Rights Movement, but for others, especially those young African-American women and men who had been directly involved in Civil Rights protests, the March on Washington, was, in Malcolm X's words, a "Farce on Washington." Those who feel this way, point to the fact that John Lewis' speech was "sanitized" to omit strong criticism of the Kennedy administration, and that, in general, the March became a public-relations activity to garner support for Kennedy's Civil Rights Bill.

(1963) W.E.B. DuBois dies in Accra, Ghana, before the March on Washington takes place.

(1963) Four African-American children are killed in a bombing of a black church in Birmingham, Alabama.

(1963) Floyd McKissick, is elected to head CORE; McKissick has more in common with nationalist politics of Malcolm X than he does with the integrationist politics of the nonviolent movement.

(1963) John Lewis is elected as third national chairman of SNCC. During Lewis' tenure as national chairman, which lasted from 1963-66, SNCC's budget goes from $250,000 to almost one million dollars.

(1963) SNCC criticizes Martin Luther King, Jr. for dismissing Jack O'Dell after the FBI reveals that O'Dell has published Communist material.

(1963) Over 200,000 students boycott Chicago schools to protest de facto school segregation.

(1963) Locked out of the "normal" electoral process, over 90,000 African-Americans in Mississippi participate in a "mock" election in which Aaron Henry runs for governor and Edward King, a white man, runs for lieutenant governor.

(1963) Wiley Branton of the Voter Education Project notifies COFO and affiliated voter-registration leaders --Bob Moses, Aaron Henry, and others in Mississippi-- that the Voter Education Project will no longer support their efforts. While he applauds their determination and struggle, Branton feels that only Federal intervention can make the registration of African-American voters possible in Mississippi.

(1963) When President Kennedy is assassinated, many African-Americans feel that they have lost a valued friend and ally in the Civil Rights struggle.

(1963) Ralph Bunche and Marian Anderson are awarded the Medal of Freedom, the highest civilian award the government can bestow.

(1963) Daisy Bates publishes her book, **The Long Shadow,** in which she relates her role in the struggle to integrate schools in the South.

(1963) COFO decides that voter education will be the focus for 1964 and that a "summer of activity" to dramatize the problems of illiteracy, poverty, and other issues in Mississippi is needed. That "summer of activity" quickly becomes known as the **Mississippi Freedom Summer.**

(1963) John Oliver Killins publishes **And Then We Heard the Thunder.**

(1964) The call goes out from COFO, SNCC, and other organizations for volunteers to work in the **Mississippi Freedom Summer.** Many of the volunteers are white college students from colleges and universities nationwide. Some volunteers are sent back because it is felt that they are not mature enough to handle Mississippi's racism.

(1964) White Mississippians respond to the **Mississippi Freedom Summer** by deputizing white organizations, spending inordinate amounts of money on weapons, and generally behaving as if they are under siege.

(1964) President Lyndon Johnson appoints Carl T. Rowan as director of the United States Information Agency.

(1964) The 24th Amendment of the Constitution is adopted and it prohibits the "denial or abridgment" of the right to vote through the use of the poll tax and other taxes.

(1964) Austin T. Walden, an Atlanta lawyer and Civil Rights activist, becomes the first black jurist in Georgia since Reconstruction.

(1964) The idea of a grassroots political party that could unseat the white democratic party of Mississippi at the Democratic National Convention is advanced. COFO makes the decision to establish the Mississippi Freedom Democratic Party (MFDP).

(1964) Joseph L. Rauh is appointed by Bob Moses as chief counsel to the newly created MFDP.

(1964) Malcolm X ends his affiliation with the Nation of Islam.

(1964) Sidney Poitier is awarded an Oscar for his performance in "Lilies of the Field."

(1964) The MFDP sets up its Washington office. Ella Baker and several activists students--Reggie Robinson, Frank Smith, and Walter Tillow spearhead this effort.

(1964) COFO calls a press conference in Jackson, Mississippi to announce the formation of its new party.

(1964) MFDP launches its "freedom registration" drive in order to register as many of the state's 400,000 disfranchised African-Americans as possible.

(1964) Leroi Jones (Amiri Baraka) receives the Obie Award for his play **The Dutchman.**

(1964) The procedure used by white Democrats in Mississippi to select delegates to the state convention and ultimately to the national convention violates their own laws: delegate selection meetings were either not held, or African-Americans were excluded from such meetings.

(1964) James Baldwin's play, "Blues for Mr Charlie," opens on Broadway and is critical of the nonviolent approach toward social change.

(1964) Congress passes the Civil Rights Act which creates the Equal Opportunity Commission and ends discrimination in all federally assisted programs.

(1964) While driving along a country road in Georgia, Lemuel Penn is shot and killed by the Ku Klux Klan.

(1964) Although the Mississippi Secretary of State declared the MFDP illegal, the MFDP holds its own state convention to select delegates (they register over 100,000 African-American on their "freedom ballots") and conducts its business in a more democratic fashion than does the regular Mississippi democratic party. The convention selects Aaron Henry as the chairperson and Fannie Lou Hamer as the vice-chairperson, of their delegation.

(1964) Despite its adherence to the law and logic, MFDP delegates are not able to gain support at the Democratic National Convention for unseating the "regular Democratic delegation." The decision of liberal whites, mainstream Civil Rights organizations, and leaders such as Dr. King, to support a "compromise" that ignores the racism, lawlessness and brutality of white Mississippians in denying African-American's the franchise disillusioned many COFO and SNCC members. (Some historians assert that this experience was an ingredient in the resurrection of "revolutionary black nationalism.")

(1964) The bodies of three Civil Rights workers--James Cheney, Michael Schwerner, and Andrew Goodman--are found in Mississippi.

(1964) Wiley Branton reports to the Southern Education Foundation that between 1962 and 1964, over 700,000 African-Americans were added to the voting rolls throughout the South.

(1964) Dr. Martin Luther King, Jr. is awarded the Nobel Peace Prize.

(1964) Black Nationalists in Michigan involved in the Freedom Now Party place 34 independent African-Americans on the ballot.

(1964) Congress launches its "War on Poverty" by passing the Economic Opportunity Act which provides for the creation and funding of such programs as Head Start, Upward Bound, and the college work-study program.

(1964) While the **Mississippi Freedom Summer** does not resolve a range of deeply ingrained problems, it does succeed in adding more than 1,200 African-Americans to the voting rolls, and in increasing the level of education of more than 2,500 African-American high-school students. In addition, the volunteers opened and operated community centers introducing local citizens to the arts and various aspects of culture. Some volunteers, like those in the Free Southern Theater, worked to acquaint Mississippians with the beauty of their own culture.

(1964) As 1964 progresses, a nationalist thrust can be seen in both CORE and SNCC as whites are invited to leave both organizations.

(1965) President Johnson gives approval to the FBI to tap the phones of all SNCC leaders.

(1965) Daniel Patrick Moynihan, issues his controversial report, **The Negro Family: The Case for National Action.** It argues that African-American families are not stable due to the prevalence of female-headed households.

(1965) Amiri Baraka founds "Spirit House," an arts and community center in Newark, New Jersey.

(1965) While standing on a ballroom stage, preparing to deliver a speech, Malcolm X is assassinated by gunmen. (The role of the Federal government and the Nation of Islam in his death remains an intense area of debate for many activists and historians.)

(1965) Dudley Randall, an African-American librarian and translator of Russian and French, founds **Broadside Press.** Some of the most important poets of the sixties were to be associated with **Broadside.**

(1965) SCLC launches a voter registration drive in Selma, Alabama.   (Aside from the obvious desire to increase the number of eligible voters, some observers note that the credibility of SCLC and of Dr. King himself had been diminished both by the level of participation of SCLC in the Mississippi Freedom Summer, and by Dr. King's conciliatory role relative to the seating of MFDP delegates.)

(1965) Dr. King announces that he will lead a march from Selma to Montgomery, Alabama, but he is eventually persuaded to allow his lieutenants to lead the march because of the danger involved.

(1965) The Selma to Montgomery March is brutally stopped on the Edmund Pettus Bridge, located outside of Selma. Several doctors and nurses who had flown in at their own expense, attend to those who have been injured.

(1965) Dr. King decides that the march must occur, and begins to make plans for its occurrence. SNCC is skeptical about King's commitment and courage. Although President Johnson is concerned that the marchers not be injured by Alabama's state troopers and other law enforcement officials, he prefers to reach a "compromise." President Johnson gets King and the white power structure to allow the demonstrators to march across the Edmund Pettus bridge, pause, and then go back to their church. When the King-led marchers reach the bridge and are told to desist, King asks if they might pray. After the prayer, King tells the marchers to turn around and go back. They do so while singing, "Ain't Nobody Gon' Turn Us 'Round."

(1965) President Johnson meets with Governor Wallace of Alabama to encourage him to allow the Selma to Montgomery march and, in general, to move the state ahead in matters of race-relations. Judge Johnson, who had previously prevented the march, issues an order making it lawful, and further instructing the state troopers and other law officials to protect the marchers from hostile whites.

(1965) Johnson makes a plea for his Voting Rights Bill, which is ultimately passed in August of the same year.

(1965) The Black Arts Repertory School opens in Harlem under the leadership of Leroi Jones (Amiri Baraka).

(1965) Dick Gregory and James Farmer are among those arrested in a Chicago demonstration against segregated schooling.

(1965) Robert Hayden wins the Grand Prize for Poetry at the **First World African Festivals of Arts** for his collection of poetry titled, **A Ballad of Remembrance.**

(1965) "People Get Ready," a popular song by Curtis Mayfield, a "soul singer with a conscious," is representative of socially committed music that came to be a defining aspect of the sixties.

(1965) Al Bell, a minister and Civil Rights activist, becomes head of promotions at Stax records, providing a formidable entree for that recording label into the African-American community.

(1965) Thurgood Marshall is nominated to become the solicitor general of the United States.

(1965) Police arrests in Watts, California ignite the Watts racial rebellion. The National Guard is brought in to end this rebellion which leaves 34 dead, over 800 injured, more than 3,000 arrested, and well over $200 million in property losses.

(1965) The first black cabinet officer, Robert C. Weaver is appointed as secretary of Housing and Urban Development.

(1965) Arthur Goldberg, the United Nations Ambassador, meets with Dr. King, Bayard Rustin, Andrew Young, and Bernard Lee to assure them that President Johnson intends to end U.S. involvement in the Vietnam war.

(1965) Constance Baker Motley is elected president of the Borough of Manhattan.

(1965) One of the men responsible for the death of Viola Liuzzo, a white Detroit housewife who participated in the Selma demonstrations, is convicted of the charge of violating her civil rights.

(1965) The whites accused of murdering the Reverend James Reeb, an African-American minister from Boston, are freed by an Alabama jury.

(1965) Ron Karenga's US, an African-American "cultural nationalist" organization, which created the doctrine of Kawaida, is formed.

Phase Two: 1966-1969
The Black Power Movement
and Nationalism

(1966) SNCC denounces American involvement in the Vietnam War, thereby becoming the first Civil Rights group to denounce the war.

(1966) Dr. King and his family move into a tenement slum on Hamlin Avenue in Chicago in order to illustrate substandard living conditions for African-Americans in Chicago. King is in and out of Chicago for the next several months, participating in the Memphis to Jackson March, as well as other activities.

(1966) For his criticism of the war in Vietnam and his association with SNCC, Julian Bond is denied his seat in the Georgia Legislature. The Supreme Court later ordered that Bond be seated.

(1966) Constance Baker Motley appointed Federal judge by President Johnson.

(1966) The U.S. government launches **Project 100,000**, a program meant to induct and train men who had been previously rejected for military service because of low educational scores. Most of these draftees are African-American and are never trained for employment in a peacetime economy. Military officials finally admit that the project was a "ruse" intended to enlarge the pool of eligible draftees.

(1966) Andrew F. Brimmer is appointed the first African-American governor of the Federal Reserve Board.

(1966) Dr. King visits with the Honorable Elijah Muhammad to

41

encourage the participation of the Black Muslims in the housing struggle. Elijah Muhammad declines.

(1966) Dr. Margaret Walker Alexander presents the novel **Jubilee** as her Ph.D. dissertation at the University of Iowa. (The novel has since been through several printings, and has been translated into several different languages.)

(1966) Marian Wright Edelman is admitted to the Mississippi bar, thereby becoming the first African-American woman there to achieve that status.

(1966) Stokely Carmichael is elected to head SNCC; Ruby Doris Robinson is elected as executive secretary.

(1966) The Lowndes County (Alabama) Freedom Organization is founded. The "Black Panther" is their symbol.

(1966) James Meredith is shot while marching from Memphis, Tennessee, to Jackson, Mississippi, and there is an immediate and profound outcry from the Civil Rights community. The decision is made to complete the march.

(1966) During the course of the march, Atlanta activist Willie Ricks promoted the slogan, "Black Power." After being arrested in Greenwood, Mississippi, Carmichael tells those on the march that he is not going to jail anymore and that what they have to start saying is "Black Power."

(1966) Louis Lomax's book, **The Negro Revolt** wins second prize for reporting at the **First World Festival of Negro Arts** in Dakar, Senegal.

(1966) Chicago obtains a Federal grant to improve substandard housing, but Dr. King asserts that the grant is too little, too late, and then proceeds to lead a procession to post demands on the door of city hall. He rides in an air-conditioned limousine. This choice does not help his credibility among the "militants."

(1966) NAACP president Roy Wilkins denounces the term "Black Power," saying that it means "anti-white power" and is, ultimately, "reverse Hitler, reverse Ku Klux Klan."

(1966) CORE's convention illustrates the extent to which the organization had become associated with Black Power. Floyd McKissick, Fannie Lou Hamer, Lonnie Shabazz, are all speakers at the convention (McKissick is the president), and they all advocate Black Power.

(1966) White politicians, including Robert Kennedy, President Johnson, and Vice President Humphrey, unilaterally denounce Black Power; other African-American politicians warn against Black Power, calling it "nihilistic" and a descent into "chaos."

(1966) The National Baptist Convention, a black religious organization, denounces Black Power.

(1966) A weeklong racial rebellion erupts in the Hough section of Cleveland, Ohio. All together, there are more than 43 racial rebellions and so-called civil disturbances in 1966.

(1966) According to articles in **U.S. News and World Report, Newsweek**, as well as articles written by Wallace Terry (the author of the 1984 publication **Bloods**), most African-Americans who are fighting in Vietnam, feel that the war is justifiable. Indeed, some condemn Stokely Carmichael and Dr. King for their criticism of the war.

(1966) **Newsweek** reports that only 35% of the African-American community oppose the war in Vietnam.

(1966) The Black Panther Party is founded in Oakland, California.

(1966) Edward Brooke of Massachusetts is the first African-American elected to the United States Senate.

(1966) John Lewis and Charles Sherrod quit SNCC because they do not like the Black Power focus.

(1966) A racial rebellion in Nashville, Tennessee, coincides with a Stokely Carmichael speech at Vanderbilt University (also in Nashville), leading Tennessee legislators to call for Carmichael's deportation to his native Trinidad.

(1967) In Chicago, Conrad Kent Rivers, Hoyt Fuller and others establish the Organization of Black American Culture; an organization that played a key role in the development of a number of African-American writers.

(1967) Leroi Jones (Amiri Baraka) begins **Jihad Press.**

(1967) FBI director, J. Edgar Hoover authorizes the infiltration and disruption of all Black Power organizations, including the Black Panther Party, SNCC, the Deacons of Defense, CORE, and the Revolutionary Action Movement.

(1967) The Black Panther Party institutes its free breakfast program, and arranges for free health care for "ghetto" residents.

(1967) A Gallup Poll indicates that Dr. King is no longer among the top ten most admired Americans. (Some historians argue that this slip was an inevitable result of his shift to fundamental critiques of the American socio-political economy.)

(1967) Adam Clayton Powell, Jr. is dismissed as Chairman of the powerful House Education and Labor Committee and denied his seat in the house.

(1967) Dr. King delivers an anti-war speech in Chicago.

(1967) Harold Cruse's **The Crisis of the Negro Intellectual** is published and in it he argues that many African-American intellectuals have opted for integration instead of nationalism. (The book has become a standard reference in any discussion of African-American cultural and intellectual history.)

(1967)   John A. Williams' **The Man Who Cried I Am** is published, and it is regarded by many as a semi-biographical novel of the life of Richard Wright.

(1967)   The NAACP, Jackie Robinson, and Dr. Ralph Bunche are among the organizations and individuals critical of Dr. King for his anti-war stance.

(1967)   The term Black Power comes to mean different things to different organizations and individuals.

(1967)   Stokely Carmichael and Charles Hamilton publish their book, **Black Power.**

(1967)   H. Rap Brown is appointed chairman of SNCC.

(1967)   Police in New York City arrest sixteen members of RAM.

(1967)   The first Black Power conference is held in Newark, New Jersey at a relatively "affluent hotel" and attracts over 1,000 "middle-class black professionals." The conference ended with a call for a "fair share" of the American pie.

(1967)   The Supreme Court declares illegal the ban on interracial marriage in the case of **Loving vs. Virginia.**

(1967)   The Newark, New Jersey, racial rebellion erupts, lasting for two weeks.

(1967)   The racial rebellion in Detroit, Michigan, occurs and is among the worst in the country.

(1967)   Thurgood Marshall is appointed the first black Supreme Court Justice.

(1967)   Muhammad Ali is convicted of draft evasion and stripped of his heavyweight boxing title.

(1967)   A **Time** magazine article notes that African-American soldiers in Vietnam prefer spending their off-duty hours with other African-Americans and with the women of "Soulville" who are "dark skinned Cambodians and the daughters of the French Senegalese."

(1967) In an altercation in which a white policeman is killed, Huey Newton is shot. For his participation, Newton is sentenced to three years in prison.

(1967) Robert Clark becomes the first African-American elected to the Mississippi legislature since Reconstruction.

(1967) Richard Gordon Hatcher is elected as the first African-American mayor of Gary, Indiana.

(1967) Carl Stokes is elected as the first African-American mayor of Cleveland.

(1967) Floyd McCree is elected as the first African-American mayor of Flint, Michigan.

(1967) By the end of the year, Dr. King's position, as well as that of the SCLC changed in ways so fundamental that some begin to refer to him as a "nonviolent Malcolm X."

(1967) Students at Howard University protest course offerings and demand Black Studies.

(1968) Lucious D. Amerson, becomes the first African-American sheriff in the South (Macon County, Alabama) since Reconstruction. He is later indicted for beating a prisoner.

(1968) African-Americans in East Palo Alto, California, petition the city government to rename the city "Narobi." Their petition is not successful.

(1968) African-American track stars, Tommy Smith and John Carlos stage symbolic protests on the victory stand at the Olympics. Smith wears a black glove, black socks, and a black scarf to protest the unfair treatment of African-Americans. John Carlos, wearing a black glove on his right hand, clenches his right hand, and raises it in a "Black Power" salute.

(1968) A "disturbance" at predominantly African-American South Carolina State College results in the death of three black students who are shot by South Carolina law officials.

(1968) A Black Power conference is held in Philadelphia; one of its major sponsors is the Clairol Company, a white business.

(1968) Larry Neal and Leroi Jones (Amiri Baraka) edit the anthology **Black Fire**. This publication is a central collection of "Black Arts" essays, short stories, poetry, and drama.

(1968) The Kerner Commission reports that America is moving towards two societies, one black, one white, "separate and unequal."

(1968) King gives the keynote address on the occasion of W.E.B. DuBois birth and uses the address as an opportunity to condemn the war in Vietnam.

(1968) Dr. King is invited to participate in a strike by public works and sanitation employees in Memphis, Tennessee. The march that he and the Reverend James Lawson lead quickly turns into a racial rebellion as young African-Americans begin to chant "Black Power, Black Power."

(1968) In a speech after the march, King predicts that the public works and sanitation employees will win their struggle. He then departs from his prepared speech, and gives what many observers characterize as his own eulogy, saying "Like anybody, I would like to live a long life. Longevity has its place.. But I'm not concerned about that now..."

(1968) The Reverend Dr. Martin Luther King, Jr. is assassinated. The nation and the world are stunned.

(1968) African-Americans, angered and saddened by King's assassination, riot in Washington, D.C., Chicago, Harlem, and in many other cities.

(1968) In a speech delivered during the presidential campaign, Richard Nixon defines Black Power as Black Capitalism, thereby "co-opting" and de-politicizing a powerful concept.

(1968) The Republic of New Africa (RNA), is founded in Detroit at the National Black Government Conference. Among other proposals, the RNA wants the United States to give them the states of South Carolina, Georgia, Alabama, Louisiana, and Mississippi.

(1968) Howard University hosts a conference titled, "Towards a Black University"; the conference is attended by almost 2,000 students, scholars and activists. One of the major results of the conference is a call to distinguish Black Studies from a Black University; the former is seen as necessary on predominantly non-African-American campuses, while the latter is seen as the ideal situation.

(1968) President Johnson signs into law the Fair Housing Act, prohibiting discrimination in the sale and rental of housing.

(1968) Ralph Abernathy leads an assortment of African-Americans, Indians, Mexican-Americans, and poor whites to Washington D.C. to set up "Resurrection City," a collection of tents and shanties from which demonstrators would lobby congress for economic justice. (By most accounts, this campaign is a failure.)

(1968) Curtis Mayfield's popular song, "We're A Winner," is representative of the self-love which characterized the Black Power era.

(1968) The plans of The National Association for Radio Announcers, an African-American organization, to open its own school of broadcasting are ultimately scuttled by a variety of internal and external pressures

(1968) A racial rebellion in Cleveland leads to the death of eight African-Americans and three white policemen. Reports circulate of armed "Black Nationalists" engaged in a battle with policemen.

(1968) The U.S. Supreme Court orders Alabama to desegregate its state prisons.

(1968) African-American soldiers in Vietnam form their own self-protection organizations--the JuJus and the MauMaus--to deal with the racism of white commanding officers and their white peers.

(1968) Students at Howard University take over the administration building and demand a black-oriented curriculum.

(1968) Shirley Chisholm defeats James Farmer to become the first African-American woman to sit in Congress.

(1968) The Black Panthers have chapters in more than a dozen states, and a membership totaling almost 5,000.

(1968) Louis Stokes, the brother of the first African-American mayor of Cleveland, Carl Stokes, is elected to Congress from Ohio.

(1968) Between 1963 and 1967, African-Americans suffer more than 17% of all casualties in the Vietnam War, although they comprise 12% of the American fighting forces in Vietnam.

(1968) Phillipa Schuyler, an African-American reporter and daughter of novelist and newspaper man George Schuyler, relates her experiences as a Vietnam War correspondent during the years of 1966 to 1967 in her book, **Good Men Die.**

(1968) As a result of student protest, the first Black Studies Program in the country is established at San Francisco State University; Dr. Nathan Hare directs the program.

(1968) SNCC and the Black Panther Party enter in alliance. But after Eldridge Cleaver and some of the other members of the Black Panther Party kidnap James Forman of SNCC, the alliance is terminated.

(1968) Southern California becomes known as "the war zone" as a result of ongoing conflicts between US and the Black Panther Party. In one such conflict, two members of the Black Panther Party are killed.

(1968) Black students at Duke University seize a campus building and demand Black Studies.

(1968) Black students from Duke University and members of the community create Malcolm X Liberation University.

(1968) Students at Southern University boycott classes in support of the wage demands of striking cafeteria workers.

(1969) Ronald Reagan, the governor of California, fires Professor Angela Davis because of her membership in the United States Communist Party.

(1969) The Institute for the Black World, an independent research and education organization, is founded in Atlanta, Georgia.

(1969) The Supreme Court rules that cities can not discriminate by enacting restrictive legislation.

(1969) The Danforth Foundation funds a Black Studies Fellowship program designed to provide Black Studies scholars with a year of study at a "prestigious university".

(1969) The Black World Foundation is established with Dr. Nathan Hare as its president. The first issue of its journal, **The Black Scholar**, is published.

(1969) The decision of Antioch College to exclude whites from its African-American Studies courses on the grounds that their "backgrounds were not relevant," is upheld by the Department of Health, Education and Welfare.

(1969) Armed African-American students take over Willard Straight Hall at Cornell University, demanding a variety of actions to improve and make meaningful their stay at Cornell. One result of their "takeover" is the creation of the Africana Studies and Research Center at Cornell.

(1969) Toni Morrison's first novel, **The Bluest Eye** is published, and it explores the self-hatred of a young black girl--Pecola Breedlove--who wishes to look like Shirley Temple.

(1969) Malcolm Bailey's exhibit, **Separate But Equal,** which is his artistic statement on the nineteenth-century slave trade, is the first exhibit at New York's Cinque Gallery.

(1969) Cecil Brown's novel, **The Life and Loves of Mr. Jiveass Nigger,** attacks the racial stereotyping of African-Americans by white authors and filmmakers. In some ways, his novel is a precursor to Robert Townsend's movie, "Hollywood Shuffle."

(1969) James Earl Ray is sentenced to 99 years in prison for the assassination of the Reverend Dr. Martin Luther King, Jr.

(1969) The U.S. Department of Labor issues guidelines for Minority employment on federally assisted construction projects.

(1969) Bobby Seale's arrest for the death of Alex Rackley continues the trend of FBI harassment of the Black Panthers.

(1969) Dwight Johnson, a black Detroiter, wins the Congressional Medal of Honor for his heroism in Vietnam. Prior to the award, Johnson is unable to find employment; after the award, several private and public businesses and agencies offer him employment. He has trouble handling his new-found success, and puts himself in a position to be killed when he attempts robbing a convenience store. A psychologist who has been counseling him, says that Johnson suffered from "post-Vietnam adjustment problems."

(1969) **Newsweek** reports that 56% of the African-American community opposes the war in Vietnam.

(1969) Harvard establishes an Afro-American Studies Program.

(1969) James Charles Evers, brother of slain Civil Rights leader Medgar Evers, is elected mayor of Fayette, Mississippi, thereby becoming the first African-American leader of a racially mixed southern town since Reconstruction.

(1969) Fred Hampton and Mark Clark, Black Panther leaders in Illinois, are killed while sleeping by Chicago policemen.

(1969) James Forman, along with other Black Power advocates, writes the Black Manifesto in which they demand reparations from white churches: $200 million for the establishment of a Southern land bank; $130 million for the creation of a black university in the South; and $20 million for the creation of black cooperative businesses.

(1969) Jewish and Catholic synagogues and churches ignore the Manifesto, but some Protestant churches do increase their contributions to African-American causes, though not necessarily through the organization that Forman and his followers created for that purpose.

(1969) In calling a meeting of all nine African-American Congressmen, Representative Charles Diggs lays the foundation for the formation of the Congressional Black Caucus.

(1969) Marvin Gaye's "What's Goin' On" is released and becomes a standard of what some in the music industry call a "concept album."

Phase Three: 1970-1974
Consolidating Gains,
and Minimizing Loses

(1970) Melvin Van Peebles releases his "Sweet Sweetback's Badass Song," ushering in what some call the "Blaxploitation Era."

(1970) Mari Evans' collection of poetry, **I am a Black Woman,** is published.

(1970) Sonia Sanchez publishes her collection of poetry, **We are a BaddDDD people.**

(1970) The Congress of African People holds its national convention in Atlanta, Georgia. Proceedings from the conference are published in 1972, entitled, **African Congress: A Documentary of the First Modern Pan African Congress.**

(1971) Jesse Jackson forms Operation PUSH (People United to Save Humanity).

(1971) The Congressional Black Caucus is founded.

(1971) Mayor Richard Gordon Hatcher convenes a meeting in Northlake, Illinois, which lays the foundation for the Gary Convention of 1972.

(1971) The Congressional Black Caucus investigates the treatment of African-American soldiers fighting in Vietnam and find that they are victims of racist actions on the part of white commanding officers and peers and that the soldiers are subject to harsh treatment for "Black Power" activities.

(1971) Amiri Baraka publishes **Raise Race Rays Raze: Essays Since 1965.**

(1971) The Harvard Business School surveys African-American deejays and program directors. The resulting report is a basis for increased involvement of such mainline recording labels as CBS in the production and distribution of African-American music.

(1971) The Federal Bureau of Investigation raids the offices of the Republic of New Africa in Jackson, Mississippi.

(1971) The Black Liberation Army is formed.

(1972) **Black Books Bulletin** begins publication. It is a publication of Don L. Lee's **Institute for Positive Education.**

(1972) The National Black Political Convention is held in Gary, Indiana. It is the most representative political event of the Black Power era.

(1972) Shirley Chisholm runs for the presidency and is disturbed that her candidacy is not considered by delegates at the National Black Political Convention.

(1972) Many Black Elected Officials who attended the Gary Convention ignore the directives and thrusts of that convention when they reach Miami, Florida--the site of the Democratic National Convention. This group of Black Elected Officials align themselves with traditional candidates in the Democratic Party.

(1972) Motown releases "It's Nation Time, African Visionary Music," an album featuring poetry by Amiri Baraka and music by a variety of notable jazz musicians such as Gary Bartz and Lonnie Liston Smith.

(1972) African Liberation Day mobilizes over 50,000 people in support of liberation struggles in Africa.

(1973) The African Liberation Support Committee raises over $40,000 in support of African liberation struggles.

(1973) U.S. troops leave Vietnam.

(1973) Ideological differences between revolutionary and cultural nationalists resurface in intense and sometimes bitter debate carried out in the pages of such journals as **The Black Scholar.**

(1974) The Little Rock Political Convention is held, and many Black Elected Officials stay away--a marked contrast to the Gary Convention held in 1972.

BIBLIOGRAPHY

The bibliography is organized into five areas: General References; Education; History and Literature; Economics; and Activism and Social Analysis.

The references are weighted toward periodical literature because it is the intent of the chronology to give the reader a sense of immediacy. Periodical literature, particularly journalism, often carries with it the preoccupations and prejudices of the era in which it is produced.

The bibliography is not exhaustive, but it does provide a reasonable representation of the era.

General References

Adams, Russell L. **Great Negroes Past and Present,** Chicago: Afro-Am Publishing, 1969.

Barker, Lucius and Jesse McCorry, Jr. **Black Americans and the Political System,** Cambridge, Ma: Winthrop Publishing, Inc., 1976.

Bennet, Lerone. **The Shaping of Black America.** Chicago: Johnson Publishing, 1975.

Blassingame, John. **New Perspective on Black Studies,** Chicago: University of Illinois Press, 1973.

Brisbane, Robert. **Black Activism.** Valley Forge, Penn.: Judson Press, 1974.

Brown, H. Rap. **Die Nigger Die.** New York: Dial Press, 1969.

Carmichael, Stokely and Charles Hamilton. **Black Power.** New York: Vintage Books, 1967.

Carson, Clayborne. **In Struggle.** Cambridge, Mass.: Harvard University Press, 1981.

Clark, Kenneth, ed. **The Negro Protest.** Boston: Harper Press, 1973.

Cruse, Harold. **The Crisis of the Negro Intellectual.** New York: William Morrow & Co., 1968.

DuBois, W.E.B. **Dusk of Dawn.** New York: Schocken Books, rpt., 1968.

Forman, James. **The Making of Black Revolutionaries.** New York: Macmillan, 1972.

Frazier, E. Franklin. **Black Bourgeoisie.** New York: Collier Books, 1962.

Gayle, Addison, ed. **The Black Aesthetic.** New York: Doubleday, 1971.

Harley, Charon and Tarborg-Penn, Rosalyn, eds. **Afro-American Women, Struggles and Images.** Post West: National University, 1978.

Harris, Norman. **Connecting Times: The Sixties in Afro-American Fiction.** Jackson, Miss.: University Press of Mississippi, 1988.

Holden, Matthew Jr. **The Politics of the Black Nation.** New York: Chandler Publishing Company, 1973.

Hornsby, Alton., Jr. **The Black Almanac. Fourth Revised Edition.** New York; Barron's Educational Series, Inc. 1977.

Jones, Leroi and Larry Neal, eds. **Black Fire.** New York: William Morrow, 1968.

Malcolm X with Alex Haley. **The Autobiography of Malcolm X.** New York: Grove Press, 1965.

Marable, Manning. **From the Grassroots: Social and Political Essays towards Afro-American Liberation.** Boston: South End Press, 1980.

Marine, Gene. **The Black Panthers.** New York: New American Library, 1969.

Morris, Milton. **The Politics of Black America.** New York: Harper & Row Publishers, 1975.

Muhammad, Elijah. **Message to the Black Man in America.** Chicago: Muhammad's Temple of Islam, No. 2, 1965.

Newton, Huey. **To Die for the People.** New York: Random

House, 1972.

Obadele, Imari. **Foundations of the Black Nation.** Detroit: Songhay Press, 1975.

Pinkney, Alphonso. **Red, Black and Green: Black Nationalism in the United States.** New York: Cambridge University Press, 1976.

Robinson, A.L. ed. **Black Studies in the University.** New Haven, Conn.: Yale University Press, 1969

Seale, Bobby. **Seize the Time.** New York: Random House, 1970.

Sellers, Cleve. **There Is a River.** New York: Harcourt, Brace, Jovanovich, 1972.

Southern, Eileen. **The Music of Black Americans.** New York: W.W. Norton, 1971.

Stone, Chuck. **Black Political Power in America,** New York: Dell Publishing, 1970.

Walton, Hanes Jr. **Black Political Parties.** New York: Free Press, 1972.

Williams, Robert. **Negroes With Guns.** Chicago: Third World Press, 1973.

Zinn, Howard. **SNCC. The New Abolitionists.** Boston: Beacon Press, 1964.

Education

A. Phillip Randolph Educational Fund. **Black Studies: Myths and Realities.** New York: A. Phillip Randolph Educational Fund, 1969.

Ahmad, Muhammad.   "On the Black Student Movement, 1969-70," **The Black Scholar** (May/June 1978), 2-11.

Allen, Robert.   "Politics of the Attack on the Black Studies," **The Black Scholar,** (September 1974), 2-7.

Blake, Elias, Jr., and Henry Cobb. **Black Studies: Issues in Their Institutional Survival.** Washington, D.C.:   Institute for Service to Education, 1976.

Blassingame, John W., ed.   **New Perspectives on Black Studies.** Urbana: University of Illinois Press, 1971.

Brown, Roscoe C.   "The White University Must Respond to Black Students' Needs," **Negro Digest** (March 1968), 24-32.

Butler, Johnnella E.   **Black Studies: Pedagogy and Revolution, a Study of Afro-American Studies and the Liberal Arts Tradition: The Discipline of Afro-American Literature.** Washington, D.C.:   University Press of America, 1981.

Coleman, Milton R.   "A Cultural Approach," **Negro Digest** (March 1969), 33-38.

Cortada, Rafael L. **Black Studies: An Urban and Comparative Curriculum.** Lexington, Ma: Xerox College Publishing, 1974.

Daniel, Philip T. K. "Black Studies: Discipline or Field of Study?", **The Western Journal of Black Studies,** 4, 3 (Fall 1980), 195-199.

Daniel, Philip T.K. and Admash Zike. **Black Studies Four Year College and University Survey.** Dekalb, Il.:   National

Council for Black Studies, 1983.

Edwards, Harry. **Black Studies.** New York: The Free Press, 1970.

Fisher, Walter. **Ideas for Black Studies.** Baltimore: Morgan State College Press, 1971.

Ford, Nick Aaron. **Black Studies: Threat-or-Challenge.** Port Washington: Kennikat Press, 1973.

Foster, Julian and Durward Long, eds. **Protest: Student Activism in America.** New York: William Morrow, 1970.

Frye, Charles A. **The Impact of Black Studies on The Curricula of Three Universities.** Washington, D.C.: University Press of America, 1976.

_____. **Towards a Philosophy of Black Studies.** San Francisco: R & E Research Associates, 1978.

Giles, Raymond H., Jr. **Black Studies Program in Public Schools.** New York: Praeger Publishers, 1974.

Goldstein, Rhoda L. **The Status of Black Studies Programs at American Colleges and Universities.** Washington, D.C.: United States Department of Health, Education, and Welfare, 1972.

Gordon, Vivian Verdell, Editor. **Lectures: Black Scholars on Black Issues.** Washington, D.C.: University Press of America, 1979.

Hare, Nathan. "What Should Be the Role of Afro-American Education in the Undergraduate Curriculum?" **Liberal Education,** (March 1969), 42-50.

_____. "The Battle for Black Studies," **The Black Scholar** (May 1972), pp. 32-47.

Harris, William H. and Darrell Millner, eds. **Perspectives on Black Studies.** Washington, D.C.: University Press of America, 1977.

Harvard University, Faculty of Arts and Sciences. **Standing Committee to Develop the Afro-American Studies Department: A Progress Report.** Cambridge, Ma.: Harvard University, September 1969.

Ijere, Martin. "Whether Economics in a Black Studies Program?", **Journal of Black Studies** (December 1972), 131-140.

Introduction To Afro-American Studies. Chicago: People's College Press, 1977.

Jablonsky, Adelaide. **Media for Teaching Afro-American Studies, IRCD Bulletin.** New York: Columbia University, Clearinghouse on the Urban Disadvantaged, Vol. 6, Nos. 1 & 2, September 1970.

Jackson, Maurice. "Towards a Sociology of Black Studies," **Journal of Black Studies** (March 1970), 131-140.

Jones, Reginald L., ed. **Black Psychology.** New York: Harper & Row, Publishers, 1972.

Karenga, Maulana Ron. "Which Road: Nationalism, Pan-Africanism, Socialism?" **The Black Scholar** (October 1974), 21-31.

Kilson, Martin. "Reflections on Structure and Content in Black Studies," **Journal of Black Studies** (March 1973), 297-314.

Madhubuti, Haki. "The Latest Purge," **The Black Scholar** (September 1974), 43-56.

McEvoy, James and Abraham Miller, eds. **Black Power and Student Rebellion.** Belmont, Ca.: Wadworth Publishing, 1969.

McWorter, Gerald A. ed. **Philosophical Perspective in Black Studies.** Urbana, IL: Afro-American Studies and Research Programs, University of Illinois, 1982. 5 vols.

_____. "Struggle Ideology and the Black University," **Negro Digest,** (March 1969), pp. 15-22.

Newton, James E. **A Curriculum Evaluation of Black Studies in Relation to Student Knowledge of Afro-American History and Culture.** San Francisco, Ca: R & E Research Associates, 1976.

New York (City) Board of Education. **Black Studies: Related Learning Materials and Activities for Kindergarten, Grade 1 and Grade 2.** New York: Board of Education, Bureau of Curriculum Development, 1970.

Orum, Anthony M. **Black Students in Protest: A Study of the Origins of the Black Student Movement.** Washington, D.C.: American Sociological Association, 1972.

Robinson, Armstead, et al. **Black Studies in the University.** New York: Bantam Books, 1969.

Salaam, Kalamu Ya and Mark Smith "Black Scholar Debate, Responses to Haki R. Madhubuti," **The Black Scholar** (January 1975), 40-53.

Simpkins, Edward. "Black Studies--Here to Stay?," **Black World** (March 1974), 26-29.

Turner, James and Eric W. Perkins. "Towards a Critique of Social Science," **The Black Scholar** (April 1976), 2-11.

Walters, Ronald, S.E. Anderson, and Alonzo. "Black Scholar Debate, Responses to Haki R. Madhubuti," **The Black Scholar** (October 1974), 47-53.

Wright, Stephen. "Black Studies and Sound Scholarship," **Phi Delta Kappan** (March 1970), 365-368.

Economics

Anderson, Talmadge. "Black Economic Liberation Under Capitalism," **The Black Scholar** (October 1970), 11-14.

Berman, Jeffery A. "The Birth of a Black Businessman." **Harvard Business Review** (September/October 1970), 48, 4-6+.

"Birth Pangs of Black Capitalism. **Time**, (October 18, 1968), 98-99.

"Black Business, Bleak Business." **Nation** (September 15, 1969), 243-245.

"Black Capitalism: What Is It?" **U.S. News And World Report** (September 30, 1968), 64-65.

"Black Capitalism." **Time** (August 15, 1969), 71.

"Black Capitalism: A Study in Frustration." **Newsweek** (September 28, 1970), 70-2.

"Black Capitalism: Into the Big Leagues." **Time** (July 25, 1969), 70.

"Black Capitalism - It Offers Little." **U.S. News and World Report** (January 12, 1970), 9.

"Black Capitalism Now: Success or Failure." **U.S. News And World Report** (November 23, 1970), 38-41.

"Black Capitalism at Work." **U.S. News And World Report** (February 17, 1969), 60-67.

"Black Capitalism-What is it?" **U. S. News And World Report** (September 30, 1968), 64-65.

Booker, Simeon. "Black Business Is Tops In South." **Ebony** (August 1971), 56-60+.

"Drive to Set Negroes Up in Business." **U.S. News and World Report** (August 31, 1964), 82.

"Economics Of Liberation." **EBONY** (August 1969), 150-154.

Frankel, Charles L. "The Uphill Road to Back Capitalism." **Nation's Business** (December 1970), 60-62.

How Negroes Can Get Ahead. **U.S. News And World Report)** (January 29, 1968), 16.

"Is Black Capitalism a Mistake." **Time** (January 12, 1970), 66-67.

"Negro Businessman: Need For Help." **Nation's Business** (August 1968), 50-54.

"New Aid for Negro Capitalists." **U.S. News And World Report** (August 26, 1968), 79.

"Of Dollars and Sense." **Ebony** (July 1964), 64.

"Profit Versus Pride: The Trouble With Capitalism." **Nation's Business** (May 1969), 78-79.

"Putting Blacks In The Black. **Nation's Business** (December 1968), 58-60.

Scott, Ann. "Report from Detroit." **Fortune** (February 1970), 71-72.

"The Beginnings of Black Capitalism." **Time** (April 6, 1970), 95-96.

"The Black and the Green." **Forbes** (September 15, 1970), 45-48.

"The Seeds for Black Capitalism." **Business Week** (November 15, 1969), 40-41.

"Training the Hardcore for Private Jobs" **U.S. News and World Report** (February 12, 1968), 60-62.

"Vitalize Black Enterprise." **Harvard Business Review** (September 1968), 88-99.

"What Ever Became of Black Capitalism." **Fortune** (August 1970), 197-198.

"Where Negro Business Gets Credit?" **Business Week** (June 8, 1968), 98-100.

Wright, Robert E. "Black Capitalism-Toward Controlled Development of Black America." **Negro-Digest** (December 1969), 27-33.

History and Literature

Archer, Douglas. "The Afro-Americans in the Arts." **Political Affairs, Theoretical Journal of the Communist Party, U.S.A.**, XLVII, 2 (1968), 74-80.

Arnez, Nancy I. "Black Poetry: A Necessary Ingredient for Survival and Liberation." **Journal for Black Studies**, XI, 1 (Sept, 1980), 3-21.

"Artist in an Age of Revolution: A Symposium." **Arts in Society**, V, 2 (1968), 219-37.

Chapman, Abraham. "Black Poetry Today." **Arts in Society**, V, 3 (1968), 401-36.

Dixon, Melvin. "Black Theater: The Aesthetics." **Negro Digest,** (July 1969), 41-44.

Dent, Tom. "The Free Southern Theater, An Evaluation," **Freedomways**, (Winter 1966), 26-30.

Fowler, Carolyn. **Black Arts and Black Aesthetics.** Atlanta, Georgia: First World Foundation, 1976.

Fuller, Hoyt W. "A Survey: Black Writers Views on Literary Lions and Values." **Negro Digest** (January 1968), 10-48, 81-88.

Gayle, Addison. "Politics of Revolution: Afro-American Literature." **Black World** (June 1972), 4-12.

Gerald, Carolyn F. "The Black Writer and His Role." **Negro Digest** (January 1969), 42-48.

Henderson, Stephen E. "Survival Motion: A Study of the Black Writer and the Black Revolution in America." **The Militant Black Writer in Africa and the United States.** Eds. cook, Mercer, and Stephen E. Henderson. Madison: University of Wisconsin

Press, 1969, pp.65-129.

Karenga, Ron. "Ron Karenga and Black Cultural Nationalism. **Negro Digest**, XVII, 3 (Jan. 1968), 5-9.

Kent, George. **Blackness and the Adventure of Western Culture.** Chicago: Third World Press, 1972.

Kgositsile, Keorapetse William. "Is the Black Revolutionist a Phony?" **Negro Digest**, XVI, 9 (1967), 9-15.

Killens, John Oliver. "The Black Writer and Revolution." **Arts in Society**, V, 3 (1968), 395-436.

Kofsky, Frank. **Black Nationalism and the Revolution in Music.** New York: Merit, Pathfinder Press, 1970.

Levesque, George A. "Black Culture, the Black Aesthetic, Black Chauvinism: A Mild Dissent." **The Canadian Review of American Studies**, XII, 3 (Winter 1983), 275-85.

Lincoln, C. Eric. "The Black Revolution in Cultural Perspective." **Union Seminary Quarterly Review**, XXIII, 3 (Spring 1968), 219-47.

Mackey, N. "Ishmael Reed and the Black Aesthetic." **CLA Journal.** (March 1978), 355-366.

Marden, Charles F. and Gladys Meyer. "The Black Challenge." **Minorities in American Society.** New York: Van Nostrand, 1978.

Mkalimoto, Ernest. "Theoretical Remarks on Afro-American Cultural Nationalism." **Journal of Ethnic Studies**, II, 2 (1974), 1-10.

Neal, Larry. "Any Day Now: Black Art and Black Liberation." **Ebony** (Augutst 1969), 54-62.

_____. "The Black Arts Movement." **The Black**

American Writer, ed. C.W.E. Bigsby. Baltimore: Penguin Books, 1971.

_____. "Film and the Black Cultural Revolution." **Arts in Society,** 2 (1968), 348-50.

_____. "The Ethos of the Blues," **The Black Scholar,** (Summer, 1972), 42-48.

Ofari, Earl. "The Emergence of Black National Consciousness in America," **Black World** (February 1971), 75-86.

Parks, Carolyn A. "Self-Determination and the Black Aesthetic: An Interview with Max Roach," **Black World** (November 1973), 62-74.

Perkins, W. E. and J. E. Higginson. "Black Students: Reformists or Revolutionaries." **The American Revolution.** Ed. Roderick Aya and Norman Miller. New York: Free Press, 1971.

Rosenthal, Joel. "Southern Black Student Activism: Assimilation vs. Nationalism." **Journal of Negro Educations,** XLIV, 2 (Spring 1975), 113-29.

Valenti, Suzanne. "The Black Diaspora: Negritude in the Poetry of West Africans and Black Americans." **Phylon, The Atlanta University Review of Race and Culture,** XXXIV, 4 (1973), 390-8.

Activism and Social Analysis

Alkalimat, Abdul Hakumu Ibn. "The Ideology of Black Social Science," **The Death of White Sociology.** New York: Random House, 1973, edited by Joyce Ladner.

Allen, Robert L. **Black Awakening in Capitalist America,** New York: Anchor Books, 1970.

"Amendment by Civil Disobedience." **National Republic,** (April 6, 1965), 268-269.

"And Then There Were None." **Time** (1970, April 27), 28.

Anthony, Earl. **Picking Up the Gun: A Report on the Black Panthers.** New York: Dial Press, 1970.

Asante, Molefi. **The Afro-Centric Idea.** Philadelphia: Temple University Press, 1987, revised edition.

Baker, Vincent S. "Negroes and the G.O.P.: Black Americans Want In". **National Review** (August 25, 1970), 892-893.

Baraka, Amiri. "Towards Ideological Clarity." **Black World,** (November 1974), 24-40.

Barbour, Floyd B., ed. **Black Power Revolt: A Collection of Essays.** Boston: Extending Horizons Books, 1968.

"Black Power." **The New Republic** (18 June 1966), 5-6.

"Black Power at the Polls." **Ebony** (January 1968), 21-28.

"Black Power in the Red." **Time** (8 July 1966), 21.

"Black Revolution-Theme in Newark." **U.S. News and World Report** (31 July 1967), 31.

"Black Power: Tool for the Communists?" **U.S. News and World Report** (15 January 1968), 14.

"Black Manifesto." **The Citizen**, (July-August 1969), 5-21.

"Black Militants Talk to Guns and Guerrillas." **U.S. News and World Report** (7 August 1967), 32.

Bloice, Carl. "On Black Self-Determination." **Political Affairs, Theoretical Journal of the Communist Party, U.S.A.**, XLVIII, 1 (1969), 59-60.

_____. "The Status of Black Liberation." **Political Affairs, Theoretical Journal of the Communist Party, U.S.A.**, XLVII, 2 (February 1968), 64-73.

Bennet, Lerone Jr. "SNCC: Rebels with a Cause." **Ebony** (July 1965), 146-153.

Booker, Simeon. "How Republican Leaders View the Negro?" **Ebony**, 19 (March 1964), 25-38.

Boskin, Joseph. "The Revolt of the Urban Ghettos, 1964-1967." **Annals of the American Academy of Political and Social Sciences**, CCCLXXXII (Mar. 1969), 1-14.

Brokckride, Wayne E. and Robert L. Scott. "Stokely Carmichael: Two Speeches on Black Power." **The Central State Speech Journal**, XIX, I (Spring 1968), 3-13.

Brown, Harold M. with Harriet Stulman, Richard Rothstein and Rennard Davis. "Black Powerlessness in Chicago." **Transactions**, VI, 1 (November 1968), 27-33.

Burgess, Parke G. "The Rhetoric of Black Power: A Moral Demand." **The Quarterly Journal of Speech**, LIV, 2 (April 1968), 122-33.

Button, James W. **Black Violence, Political Impact of the**

1960s Riots. Princeton: Princeton University Press, 1978.

Carmichael, Stokely. **Stokely Speaks, Black Power to Pan-Africanism.** New York: Random House. 1965.

_____. "Towards Black Liberation," **Massachusetts Review** (Autumn 1966), 639-651.

_____. "We Are All Africans." **The Black Scholar** (July 1970), 15-19.

Carter, Russ. "Civil Rights Legislation in a new Administration." **The Crisis** (October 1962), 449-452.

Chambers, Ernest. "We have marched, we have cried, we have prayed." **Ebony** (April 1968), 29-38.

"Civil Rights Bill and Strategy for Passage." **Community** (February 1964), 14.

"Civil Rights Act has shaped nation's politics for 25 years." **The New York Times** (2 July 1989), sec. 1: 16.

Clark, Kenneth B. "Thoughts on Black Power." **Dissent,** XV (March-April 1968), 98 and 192.

Cleghorn, Resse. "No Seat for the Negro Who Won." **The New Republic** (29 January 1966), 11-12.

Clemners, Ernest. "We Have Marched." **Ebony** (April 1968), 29-32.

Comer, James P. "Black Rebellion: Some Parallels." **Midway,** IX, 1 (1968), 33-48.

Conyers, John. "Politics and the Black Revolution." **Ebony,** (October 1969), 162-166.

Cook, Samuel Du Bois. "The Tragic Myth of Black Power." **New South,** XXI (Summer 1966), 58-64.

Cross, William E. "The Thomas and Cross Models on Psychological Nigrescence: A Literature Review," **Journal of Black Psychology,** 4 (1978), 13-31.

Cross, William E. "Black Family and Black Identity: A Literature Review," **The Western Journal of Black Studies,** 2 (1978), 111-124.

Cruse, Harold. "Part I: Black Politics Series--The Little Rock National Convention," **Black World** (October 1974), 10-17.

_____. "The National Black Political Convention, Part II," **Black World** (November 1974), 4-23.

Current, Gloster B. "58th Annual NAACP Convention." **The Crisis** (August-September 1967), 352-360.

"Demonstrations." **Community** (November 1965), 4-8.

Dolan, Mary. "The Protest and the Backlash." **Community** (June 1964), 4-5.

Dowey, Edward A., Jr. "The Black Manifesto: Revolution, Reparations, Separation." **Theology Today,** XXVI (October 1969), 288-293.

Dratch, Howard B. "The Emergence of Black Power." **International Socialist Journal,** XXVI-XXVII (July 1968), 321-65.

"Dr. King's Policy: Invitation to Racial Violence." **U.S. News and World Report.** (4 October 1965), 22.

"Did the war on poverty fail?" **The New York Times,** 20 (August 1989), sec. 4: E23.

Duberman, Martin. "Black Power in America." **Partisan Review,** XXXV, 1 (1968), 34-48.

Editors. "Civil Rights- Where are we now?" **Black Enterprise**

(August 1983), 38-39+.

Edmondson, Locksley. "Black Power: A View from the Outside." Africa Today, XIV (December 1967), 6-9.

Fager, Charles E. White Reflections on Black Power. Grand Rapids, Mi: William B. Erdmans, 1967.

Feldman, Paul. "The Pathos of Black Power." Dissent, XIV (January-February, 1967), 69-79.

Foner, Philip S., ed. The Black Panthers Speak. The Manifesto of the Party: The First Documentary Record of the Panthers Program. New York: Lippincott, 1970.

Forman, James. "The Concept of International Black Power." Pan-African Journal, I, 203 (1968), 92-5.

Franklin, Raymond S. "The Political Economy of Black Power." Social Problems, XVI, 3 (1969), 386-301.

Genovese, Eugene D. "The Influence of the Black Power Movement on Historical Scholarship: Reflections of a White Historian." Daedalus, LXXXXIX, 2 (Spring 1970), 473-94.

Gill, Robert L. and Roberta L. Gill. "International Implications of Black Power as Viewed by Their Advocates." The Quarterly Review of Higher Education Among Negroes, XXXVII, 4 (Oct. 1969), 158-76.

Goldin, Greg. "Ex Parte Pratt." The Nation (28 February 1981), 229.

Golden, Harry. "Education and Politics." The Crisis (August-September 1962), 397-401.

Good, Paul. "A White Look At Black Power." The Nation (8 August 1968), 112-117.

Graham, Hugh D. "The Storm over Black Power." The

Virginia Quarterly, XXXXIII, 4 (Autumn 1967), 545-65.

Gregg, Richard B, A. J. McCormack and D. J. Pedersen. "The Rhetoric of Black Power: A Street Level Interpretation." The Quarterly Journal of Speech, LV, 2 (April 1969), 151-60.

Groves, Harry E. "The Revolt of Black Students." Journal of Human Relations, XVII, 2 (Second Quarter 1969), 185-97.

Hamilton, Charles V. "An Advocate of Black Power Defines It." The New York Times Magazine (14 April 1968), 22-23, 79-83.

Harding, Vincent. "Black Power and the American Christ." The Christian Century, LXXXIV, 1 (4 January 1967), 10-13.

_____. "The Religion of Black Power." The Religious Situation. Ed. Donald R. Cutter. Boston: Beacon Press, 1968.

Harris, Paul. "Black Power Advocacy: Criminal Anarchy or Free Speech." California Law Review, LVI (May 1968), 702-55.

Harris, Janet and Julius W. Hobson. Black Pride: A People's Struggle. New York: McGraw Hill, 1969.

Haskins, James. Profiles in Black Power. Garden City, NY: Doubleday, 1972.

Hawkins, Russell. "What Black Power Leaders Are Demanding." U.S. News and World Report (August 7, 1967), 63:32.

"Heavy Baggage." Nation (20 July 1970), 37.

Heresi, Dennis. "Huey Newton Symbolized the Rising Black Anger of a Generation." The New York Times 138 (August 23, 1989), B7.

Hostetter, Robert. "Leo Holt: Portrait of an Independent

Candidate." **Community** (February 1967), 11

Houlding, Andrew. "The Paranoids Were Right." **Harpers Magazine**, 267 (September 1983), 29.

Hunt, James D. "Gandhi and the Black Revolution." **The Christian Century: An Ecumenical Weekly**, LXXXVI, 40 (1 October 1969), 1242-4.

"Inside story of 'Black Power' and Stokely Carmichael." **U.S. News & World Report** (15 August 1966), 12.

"Is It really necessary?" **Community**, (May 1964), 10.

"If Kennedy Hadn't Picked LBJ." **U.S. News and World Report** (2 August 1965), 50.

Jackson, James E. "On Self-Determination--Separatism--A Bourgeoisie-Nationalist Trap." **Political Affairs, Theoretical Journal of the Communist Party, U.S.A.**, XLViii, 3 (March 1969), 25-38.

James, Andrew. "The Negro and the democrats." **Community** (October 1964), 4-5.

Joynes, Thomas J. "Negroes Identity--Black Power and Violence." **Journal of Human Relations**, XVII, 2 (Second Quarter 1969), 198-207.

"Jungle Justice for the Panthers." **America**, (30 May 1970), 573.

Killens, John Oliver, et al. "Symposium: The Meaning of Black Power." **Negro Digest**, XVI (November 1966), 20-37.

Killian, Lewis M. **The Impossible Revolution, Black Power and the American Dream**. New York: Random House, 1968.

Kilson, Martin. "Black Power: Anatomy of a Paradox." **The Harvard Journal of Negro Affairs**, II, I (1968), 30-34.

Lasch, Christopher. "Special Supplement: The Trouble with Black Power." **The New York Review of Books**, X, 4 (29 Feb. 1968), 4-14.

Lawrence, D.L. "The Wrong Way." **U.S. News and World Report** (22 March 1965), 124.

Lazarus, Simon. "Black Power?" **The New Republic**, CLVIII, 2 (13 Jan. 1968), 27-34.

"LBJ At A Low Ebb." **Newsweek** (21 August 1967), 15-17.

"LBJ Order." **U.S. News and World Report** (4 October 1966), 9.

Lester, Julius. **Look Out Whitey: Black Power's Gon Get Your Mama.** New York: Grove Press, 1968.

Lewis, Alfred Baker. "Economic Issues and the New Negro Vote." **The Crisis** (April 1966), 198-200.

_____. "State Civil Rights Gains." **The Crisis** (December 1962), 577-579.

"Let's Give Him a Chance." **Ebony** (April 1969), 52.

Lightfoot, Claude M. **Ghetto Rebellion and Black Liberation,** New York: International, 1968.

Lomax, Louis E. **The Negro Revolt.** New York: Signet Books, 1962.

Lyman. Stanford, M. "Cherished Values and Civil Rights." **The Crisis** (December 1964), 645-654, 695.

MacDonald, A. P., Jr. "Black Power." **The Journal of Negro Education,** XLIV, 4 (1975), 547-54.

Madhubuti, Haki. "Enemy: From the White Left, White Right and In Between." **Black World** (October 1974), 36-47.

_____. "Pan-Africanism--Land and Power." **The Black Scholar** (May 1970), 15-19.

Major, Reginald. **A Panther is a Black Cat.** New York: William Morrow, 1971.

Malveaux, Julianne. "Our Power To Vote In Jeopardy." **Essence** (September 1984), 170-171.

Marine, Gene. **The Black Panthers.** New York: Signet, New American Library, 1969.

McCartney, John. "Black Power: Past, Present and Future." **Forums in History.** St. Charles, Mo.: Forum Press, 1973.

McCormack, Donald J. "Stokely Carmichael and Pan-Africanism: Back to Black Power." **The Journal of Politics,** XXXV, 2 (1973), 386-409.

Meier, August and Elliot M. Rudwick, eds. **Black Protest in the Sixties.** Chicago: Quadrangle Books, 1970.

Miles, Michael. "Revolution or Reform on the Black Left." **The New Republic** (19 August 1967), 9-16.

Milstein, Tom. "A Perspective on the Panthers." **Commentary,** L, 3 (September 1970), 35-43.

"More on the Panthers." **Nation,** (29 December 1969), 717.

McLemore, Leslie B. "Mississippi Freedom Democratic Party," **The Black Politician,** 3, 2 (October 1971), 19-22.

Moon, Henry. "How We Voted and Why?" **Crisis** (January 1965), 26-31.

Moon, Henry Lee. "The pursuit of Political Parity." **The Crisis** (January 1966), 9-17.

Morsell, John A. "The Meaning of Black Nationalism." **The Crisis** (February 1962), 69-75.

Mitchell, Clarence. "Civil Rights and Economic Rights." **The Crisis** (April 1968), 117-121.

Morsell, John A. "Applicability of Civil Rights Act of 1964 to the Non-South." **The Crisis** (November 1964), 599-600.

Muse, Benjamin. **The American Negro Revolution: From Violence to Black Power, 1963-1967**. Bloomington: Indiana University Press. 1968.

Newton, Huey. "Black Panthers." **Ebony** (August 1969), 106-8.

"New Voting Rights Plan." **U.S. News and World Report**, (March 29, 1965), 33.

"Negroes: Big Gains, But still Problems." **U.S. News and World Report** (13 November 1967), 16.

"New Voting Rights Plan." **U.S. News and World Report** (29 March 1965), 33.

"Negro Tactics: Change Coming." **U.S. News and World Report**, (4 January 1966), 41.

"Official NAACP Position on Presidential Campaign." **The Crisis** (October 1964), 500-503.

Olds, Sally. "The White liberals Take a Stand." **Community** (December 1965), 9-11.

O'Keefe, Robert. "Campy Civil Rights Movements." **Community** (December 1965), 3.

Onwuachi, P. Chike. "Identity and Black Power." **Negro Digest**, XVI, 5 (March 1967), 31-37.

Osbourne, David. "Winning Battles, Losing the War: The Great Society revisited." **Mother Jones** (June 1986), 13.

"Panthers and the Law. **Newsweek** (23 February 1970), 26-30.

Palmer, L.F. "Out to Get the Panthers: FBI and Chicago Police." **Nation** (28 July 1969), 78-82.

Partee, Carter. "Incredible Malcolm X." **Community** (February 1966), 10.

Patterson, Robert B. "Voter Registration." **The Citizen** (March 1969), 14-18.

Peck, James. "Black Power: Two Views; Black Racism." **Liberation**, XI, 7 (October 1966), 31-32.

Pivan, Frances Fox and Cloward, Richard A. "Descensus Politics." **The New Republic** (20 April 1968), 2-4.

Polenberg, Richard. **One Nation Divisible: Class, Race and Ethnicity in the United States Since 1938**. New York: Viking Press, 1980.

"Power and Responsibility." **The Nation** (October 16, 1967), 356-357.

Prestage, Jewel. "Black Politics and the Kerner Report: Concerns and Directions," **Social Science Quarterly**, 49, 3 (December 1968), 453-464.

"Persecution and Assassination of the Black Panther Party as Directed by Guess Who." **National Review** (30 December 1969), 1306-7.

"Political Gains by Negroes". **U.S. News and World Report** (13 July 1970), 40-41.

"Power and Responsibility." **The Nation** (16 October 1967), 356-357.

"Race Issue: What City Voters Say Now." **U.S. News and World Report,** (16 October 1967), 35.

Reid, Inez Smith. "Black Power and Uhuru: A Challenge." **Pan-African Journal,** I, I (Winter 1968), 23-7.

Relyea, Harold C. "Black Power and Parallel Institutions: Ideological and Theoretical Considerations." **Journal of Human Relations,** XVII, 2 (Second Quarter 1969), 208-23.

Rogers, Ray. "Black Guns on Campus." **Nation** (May 5, 1969), 558-560.

"Reagan Versus LBJ." **National Review** (June 1981), 705.

Rudwick, Elliot M. "CORE: The Road from Interracialism to Black Power." **Journal of Voluntary Action Research,** I, 4 (1972), 12-9.

Rustin, Bayard. "The Myths of the Black Revolt." **Ebony,** (August 1969), 96.

Robinson, Jackie. "The G.O.P.: For White Men Only?" **Ebony** (August 1963), 10-11.

Salaam, Kalamu Ya. "Run Together Children, Don't You Get Weary." **Black Collegian** (January-February 1984), 52-54+.

Sanders, Charles et. al. "Black Power At The Polls." **Ebony,** (November 1967), 23-32.

_____. "Ambassador is a Lady." **Ebony** (January 1966), 23-25.

Sayre, Nora. "The Black Panthers Are Coming: America on the Eve of Race Revolution." **New Statesman,** LXXVII (2 May 1969), 613-616.

Schanhe, Don A. "Panthers Against the Wall." **Atlantic** (May 1970), 55-61.

Scott, Benjamin F. **The Coming of the Black Man.** Boston: Beacon Press, 1969.

Scott, Robert L. "Justifying Violence: The Rhetoric of Black Power," **The Central States Speech Journal,** XIX, 2 (Summer 1968), 97-104.

Sears, David O. "Black Attitudes Toward the Political System in the Aftermath of the Watts Insurrection." **Midwest Journal of Political Science,** XIII, 4 (November 1969), 515-44.

"Semantics of the Civil Rights Struggle." **Crisis,** (June-July 1966), 299-301.

"Some Clues to Future Policy on Racial Issues". **U.S. News and World Report** (January 6, 1967), 7.

"South's New Negro Voters: Can They Swing An Election?" **U.S. News and World Report** (23 August 1965), 38-40.

Stern, Sol. "America's Black Guerrillas." **Ramparts, VI, 4** (September 1967), 24-7.

_____. "The Call of the Black Panthers." **The New York Times Magazine** (August 6, 1967), 10-11.

_____. "Fred Hampton's Apartment." **Nation** (23 March 1970), 325-326.

Stipe, Michael. "Black Militants Talk of Guns and Guerrillas." **U.S. News and World Report** (7 August 1967), 32.

Sweetser, Thomas. "Rundown on a Demonstration." **Community** (December 1965), 4-7.

Stull, Harriet. "Postscript on the Election." **Community**

(December 1964), 8.

"Symposium: Chicago's Black Caucus." **Ramparts**, VI, 4 (1967), 99-114.

"The Rising Negro Vote." **U.S. News and World Report** (29 November 1965), 46-47.

Tolbert, Richard C. "A Key to Genuine Power: A New Brand of Black Nationalism." **Negro Digest**, XVI, 10 (1967), 19-28.

Toldson, Ivory and Alfred D. Pasteur. **Roots of Soul.** Garden City, New York: Doubleday, 1982.

Tomlinson, T. M. "Determinants of Black Power Politics: Riots and the Growth of Militancy." **Psychiatry, Journal for the Study of Interpersonal Processes**, XXXIII, 2 (1970), 247-64.

Turner, James. "Black Nationalism: The Inevitable Response." **Black World** (January 1971), 4-7.

Vivian, C. T. **Black Power and the American Myth.** Philadelphia: Fortress Press, 1970.

Wagstaff, Thomas. **Black Power: The Radical Response to White America.** Beverly Hills: Glencoe Press, 1969.

Washington, Kenneth S. "Black Power: Action or Reaction?" **American Behavioral Scientist**, XIII, 4 (1969), 47-9.

Wildavsky, Aaron. "The Empty-Head Blues: Black Rebellion and White Reaction." **The Public Interest**, II (Spring 1968), 3-16.

Wilkins, Roy. "The Civil Rights Bill of 1966." **Crisis** (June-July 1965), 302-307.

_____. "Violence Is Not The Answer." **Crisis** (May 1969), 200-205.

_____. "Civil Rights, 1963: A summary." The **Crisis**,

(February 1964), 69-71.

Williams, Franklin. "Law and Human Rights- a Comment." *Crisis* (January 1962), 10-17.

Wilson, James A. "White Power and Black Supremacy." *Pittsburgh Business Review*, XXXVII (Aug. 1967, 12-4).

Wohlstetter, Albert and Roberta Wohlstetter. "Third Worlds Abroad and at Home." *The Public Interest*, 14 (Winter 1969), 88-107.

Wright, Benjamin. "Is This Worth Fighting For?" *Crisis*, (February 1960), 80-83.

"What Does it Contain?" *Community*, (May 1964), 10.

"What the Negro Vote Will Do To South." *U.S. News and World Report* (29 March 1965), 30-32.

"What Negro Leaders Want Now". *U.S. News and World Report* (24 February 1969), 44-51.

"Why a Top Negro Agreed to Join the Nixon Team". *U.S. News and World Report* (24 February 1969), 16.

"What Black Power Leaders Are Demanding." *U.S. News and World Report*, (7 August 1967), 63.

"What the Negro Vote Will Do To The South." *U.S. News and World Report* (29 March 1965), 30-32.

"Why they Riot." *National Review* (March 1965), 178-80.

"Who will get the Negro Vote? *Ebony* (November 1960), 40-42.

Zangrando, Robert L. "From Civil Rights to Black Liberation: The Unsettled 1960s." *Current History*, LVII (November 1969), 281-286.

Glossary

Abernathy, Ralph David (1926-). A close associate of Dr. Martin Luther King, Jr., and a key member of the Southern Christian Leadership Conference. After Dr. King's assassination, Mr. Abernathy organized the Poor People's Campaign in Washington. A recent book by Abernathy concerning his relationship with Dr. King has been roundly criticized by various members of the Civil Rights community.

A. Phillip Randolph Institute. Founded in 1964 by A. Phillip Randolph, an important force in labor and employment activities, the institute does work in the area of civil rights and labor relations.

Baldwin, James (1924-1988). Novelist, essayists and civil rights activist, Baldwin's work has received international acclaim. His **The Fire Next Time**, a collection of essays published in 1963, is useful reading for individuals interested in understanding the Civil Rights Movement.

Bates, Daisy (1922-). A Civil Rights activist who played a key role in the desegregation of schools in Little Rock, Arkansas. Her book, **The Long Shadow**, discusses her life as a Civil Rights activist.

Bennett, Lerone, Jr. (1928-). A senior editor at **Ebony,** Bennet has written numerous articles and books chronicling the African-American experience.

Black Panther Party. Founded in Oakland, California, in 1966 by Bobby Seale and Huey Newton, this organization sought the self-determination and self-defense of the "oppressed black community."

Black Power. This term received widespread attention

during the 1966 "March Against Fear" between Memphis, Tennessee and Jackson, Mississippi.   Although Stokely Carmichael is the activist most often associated with the term, it had been in circulation for some time.   In general, Black Power came to mean the empowerment of African-American communities in accordance to what those communities deemed most important.

Bond, Julian (1940-   ). A member of the Student Non-Violet Coordinating Committee (1960-66), and then the Georgia House of Representatives.   Bond now works as a television commentator.

Branton, Wiley A. (1923-1988). Born in Pine Bluff, Arkansas, he was an attorney who headed the Voter Education Project of the Southern Regional Council from 1962 to 1965.   From 1965 to 1967 he was a special assistant to U.S. attorney generals Nicholas Katzenbach and Ramsey Clark.

Brown, H. Rap (1943-   ). In 1967, Brown became president of the Student Non-Violent Coordinating Committee. During the sixties, Brown was popular among many young African-Americans because of the way he delivered his message of Black Power.   His book, **Die Nigger Die!** was published in 1969.

Brown, James (1933-   ). A prolific composer, singer, and a successful businessman, Brown's music during the sixties reflected the Black Consciousness thrust of the era with such "hits" as "Say it Loud, I'm Black and I'm Proud," and "Don't Want Nobody Givin' Me Nothin', Open up the Door and I'll Get in Myself."

Carmichael, Stokely (1941-   ). Born in Port-of-Spain, Trinidad, Carmichael was a charismatic leader of SNCC (1966) during the Black Power era.   The book he co-authored with Charles Hamilton (**Black Power: The Politics of Liberation in Black AMerica**), as well as numerous articles and speeches, established Carmichael as a central force in the Black Power Movement.

Chisholm, Shirley A. (1924–   ). In 1968, Chisholm was elected to the House of Representatives from New York, thereby becoming the first African-American woman in Congress. Her unsuccessful run for the presidency in 1972 was also a first.

Congress of Racial Equality (CORE). This organization was founded in 1942 by James Farmer at the University of Chicago, and it played a key role in the early sit-in demonstrations during the first phase of the sixties.

Davis, Angela (1944–   ). A native of Birmingham, Alabama, Ms. Davis came to national attention as a result of her alleged involvement in the attempted escape of three San Quentin prisoners. Her book, **If they Come in the Morning** (1972), is standard reading for understanding the relationship of African-Americans to the criminal justice system.

Evers, James Charles (1922-   ). He assumed leadership of the Mississippi NAACP, after his brother, Medgar Evers, was assassinated. Evers was elected mayor of Fayette, Mississippi, in 1969.

Evers, Medgar Wiley (1925-1963)   Born in Decatur, Mississippi, Evers was the field secreaty of the Mississippi NAACP at the time when he was assassinated in front of his home in Jackson, Mississippi.

Farmer, James (1920-   ). Born in Marshall, Texas, Farmer created the Congress of Racial Equality (CORE) in 1942. He was active in a variety of Civil Rights struggles during the sixties. Shirley Chisholm defeated him in his 1968 run for the U.S. Congress.

Federation of Pan-African Educational Institutions. Founded in 1971, this organization was composed of six institutions: the Marcus Garvey Memorial Institute, Monrovia, Liberia; the Chad School in Newark, New Jersey; the Clifford McKissick Community School in Milwaukee, Wisconsin; the Pan African Work Center in Atlanta, Georgia; the Marcus Garvey School in

Youngstown, Ohio; and Malcolm X Liberation University in Greensboro, North Carolina. These schools were part of the continuing attempt to institutionalize the Black Power movement.

Fuller, Hoyt (1924-1981). A native of Atlanta, Georgia, Fuller edited **Negro Digest** (later renamed **Black World**), one of the most important journals of the sixties. He was also one of the founding members of the Organization of Black American Culture in Chicago. Fuller was the editor of **First World** at the time of his death.

Giovanni, Nikki (1934-   ). A native of Knoxville, Tennessee, Giovanni was one of the important poets during the sixties. Her books include **Black Feelings, Black Talk** (1968), and **My House** (1972).

Gordy, Berry (1929-   ). A native of Detroit, Michigan, Berry founded Motown Records in 1959, and produced some of the most definitive music of the era.

Gregory, Dick (1932-   ). A native of St. Louis, Missouri, Gregory first gained public attention as a comedian. He ran unsuccessfully for mayor of Chicago in 1966, and for the presidency in 1968. In 1964 he published **Nigger: An Autobiography**.

Harding, Vincent (1931-   ). Born in New York, Harding is an historian and activist. He was one of the founders of the Institute of the Black World in 1969.

Hatcher, Richard Gordon (1933-   ). Hatcher was born in Michigan City, Indiana, and became the first African-American mayor of Gary, Indiana, in 1967. He was also one of the co-conveners of the National Black Political Convention in Gary, Indiana (1972).

Jackson, George (1941-1971). A native of Chicago, Illinois, Jackson became known as a political prisoner. He entered the prison system at the age of 15 to serve a sentence of one year to life for stealing $70. His book, **Soledad Brother: The Prison**

Letters of George Jackson (1970) is important reading for understanding the relationship between African-American men and the criminal justice system. Jackson was killed while alledgedly trying to escape from prison.

Jackson, Jesse L. (1941-   ). A disciple of Dr. Martin Luther King, Jr., Jackson was involved in a range of civil rights activities: the Southern Christian Leadership Conference, the Poor People's Campaign. He founded People United to Save Humanity (PUSH). 1988 marked his second attempt to win the Democratic nomination for the presidency. While winning primary victories in Michigan, Georgia, and other states Jackson finished second to Michael Dukakis.

James Van Der Zee Institute. Founded in 1967, this institute is named for photographer James Van Der Zee and operates to preserve the photographs that Van Der Zee made of the Harlem Community during the 1920s and 30s. The Institute is representative of the Black Power era's concern to institutionalize African-American culture.

King, Martin Luther, Jr. (1929-1968). A native of Atlanta, Georgia, King is the best known civil rights activists of the sixties. His birthday (15 January) is now a national holiday.

Ku Klux Klan. Founded in Pulaski, Tennessee, in 1866, this antiblack terrorist organization is involved in a variety of violent and illegal acts intended to deny African-Americans democratic rights.

Lomax, Louis (1922-1970). Born in Valdosta, Georgia, Lomax was a journalist, and educator. Two of his most important books are **The Negro Revolt** (1962), and **When the Word is Given: A Report on Elijah Muhammad, Malcolm X, and the Black Muslim World** (1963).

Malcolm X (1925-1965). Born in Omaha, Nebraska, Malcolm X was a spokesmen for the Nation of Islam, and was one of the most important leaders of the sixties. Many African-American leaders mark his assassination in 1965 as the turning point in their political development.

Mississippi Freedom Democratic Party (MFDP). Founded in 1963, this organization worked for the inclusion of African-Americans in Mississippi politics. MFDP drew national attention when it challenged the seating of the all white Mississippi delegation to the 1964 Democratic National Convention.

Montgomery Improvement Association. Founded in 1955 by Dr. Martin Luther King, Jr., and Ralph Abernathy to coordinate the Montgomery Bus Boycott, this organization provided leadership training for a number of civil rights leaders; it also served as a model for the formation of organizations intended to end discrimination.

National Bibliographic and Research Center. This organization was founded in 1965 with the idea of furthering knowledge of the African-American experience. The organization is continuous with the institutionalization of African-American culture that was too become so prevalent after 1966.

National Black Political Convention. The first convention was held in Gary, Indiana, in 1972 with Richard G. Hatcher (former mayor of Gary), Charles Diggs (the former U.S. Congressman from Detroit), and Imamu Amiri Baraka (Leroi Jones) as conference convenors. The second convention was held in 1974. The purpose of both conventions was to advance African-American political empowerment.

National Urban League. Founded in 1910, this interracial, nonprofit organization works to secure equal opportunities for African-Americans. The Urban League issues an annual report on the "Status of Black America."

Newton, Huey (1942-1989). Newton and Bobby Seale founded the Black Panther Party in 1966. Many of the initiatives of the Black Panther Party (free lunches, medical care for inner city residents) were models for various public agencies.

Opportunities Industrialization Centers (OIC) of America. Founded in 1964 by the Reverend Leon H. Sullivan, this organization provides vocational training.

Randall, Dudley (1914–   ). Born in Washington, D.C., this poet and librarian founded Broadside Press in 1965, and during the course of the sixties it became one of the most important publishing houses of the era.

Republic of New Africa. Founded in 1968, this organization wanted to establish a separate black nation within America, consisting of the states of Alabama, Georgia, Mississippi, Louisiana, and South Carolina.

Southern Christian Leadership Conference (SCLC). Founded in 1957, this Civil Rights organization was an offshoot of the Montgomery Improvement Association. This organization was founded by Dr. King and had as its goal the full democratic rights of African-Americans.

Student Non-Violent Coordinating Committee (SNCC). Founded in 1960, in part as a student offshoot of SCLC, was initially an integrationist organization that later became a nationalist organization after 1965.

Young, Andrew, Jr. (1932–   ). A native of New Orleans, Louisiana, Young was a disciple of Dr. King. Most recently he was mayor of Atlanta, Georgia.

Index

Organization of Black American Culture (11), (42), (87)
Oscar (33)

Peoples College (15)
Phillipa Schuyler (47)
Poor People's Campaign (46), (84), (88)
President Johnson (35-37), (39), (41), (46)
President Kennedy (3), (4), (25), (27), (28), (30), (31)

Ralph Bunche (32), (43)
Reggie Robinson (33)
Resurrection City (46)
Reverend James Reeb (7), (38)
Revolutionary Action Committee (5), (29)
Revolutionary black nationalism (34)
Richard Gordon Hatcher (13), (16), (44), (51)
Richard Nixon (10), (45)
Robert C. Weaver (37)
Robert Clark (13), (44)
Robert Kennedy (29), (41)
Robert Sherrod (25)

Selma, Alabama (36)
Shirley Chisholm (13), (47), (52), (86)
Sonia Sanchez (51)
South Carolina State College (45)
Southern Christian Leadership Conference (3), (23), (84), (88),
   (90)
Southern Education Foundation (34)
Southern Regional Council (24), (25), (27), (85)
Southern University (22), (27), (48)
Spirit House (11), (35)
Stokely Carmichael (9), (19), (40-43), (69), (74), (76), (85)
Student Non-Violent Coordinating Committee (SNCC) (3), (23),
   (90)

Taconic Foundation (24), (27)
Tennessee State University (21)
The Black Scholar (18), (48), (53), (58-62), (67), (70), (76)
The Wilmington Ten (18)

Thurgood Marshall (25), (37), (43)
Tom Dent (29)

U.S. Department of Labor (49)
Unity without uniformity (1), (16)
University of Georgia (24)
University of Mississippi (24), (27), (28)
Upward Bound (6), (35)
US (10-12), (36), (38), (48)

Vanderbilt University (42)
Vietnam (1), (8), (13), (18-20), (37), (39), (41), (43), (45), (47), (49), (50), (51), (53)
Viola Liuzzo (7), (37)
Voter Education (4), (24), (25), (27), (29), (31), (32), (85)
Voter Education Project (4), (27), (29), (31), (85)
Voting Rights Bill (6), (36)

W.E.B. DuBois (26), (31), (45)
Walter Tillow (33)
War on Poverty (6), (35), (71)
Watts (12), (37), (80)
Wiley Branton (4), (31), (34)
Willie Joe Lovett (30)
Willie Ricks (9), (40)